A NEW FORMATION

A NEW FORMATION

How Black Footballers Shaped the Modern Game

EDITED BY

CALUM JACOBS

3 5 7 9 10 8 6 4

#Merky Books
20 Vauxhall Bridge Road
London SW1V 2SA

#Merky Books is part of the Penguin Random House group
of companies whose addresses can be found at
global.penguinrandomhouse.com.

First published by #Merky Books in 2022

www.penguin.co.uk

A CIP catalogue record for this book is available from
the British Library.

ISBN 9781529118704

Typeset in 10.5/14.5 pt Sabon LT Pro
by Integra Software Services Pvt. Ltd, Pondicherry

Printed and bound in Great Britain by Clays Ltd, Elcograf S.p.A.

The authorised representative in the EEA is Penguin Random House Ireland,
Morrison Chambers, 32 Nassau Street, Dublin D02 YH68.

www.greenpenguin.co.uk

Penguin Random House is committed to a sustainable future for
our business, our readers and our planet. This book is made from
Forest Stewardship Council® certified paper.

For my dad, Gregory Jacobs.

Contents

Introduction

Calum Jacobs

A New Formation should not be understood as a book about 'racism in football', a manifesto for change or a handbook about how to build allyship. You will find no blueprints, solutions or three-point plans within these pages. Although each essay, by virtue of its very existence, is advocating for a change in how Black people are perceived – both by broad sections of the media and by white society – no explicit case for change will be presented. If you are unclear about why Black people, or people of the global majority,* should not be asked to continuously make a case for racial equity, then, honestly, this book may not be for you.

None of the essays you are about to read aim to understand the individuals they're focused on solely through the trials – or racism – that they've faced, battled and overcome. To do so would strip them of their personhood and complexity, reducing them to emblems or two-dimensional symbols. That's not to say that *A New Formation* eschews discussion of anti-Black racism; it simply refuses to use it as the bedrock for its analyses.

Instead, this book pays tribute to, and details the influence of, a deliberately varied range of Black and mixed-race footballers, past and present, who have shaped 'the beautiful game' and broadened conceptions of the Black experience

* The demographic designation 'ethnic minority' is grossly inaccurate given that Black, Indigenous and people of colour comprise over eighty per cent of the world's population, making them the global majority.

through the things they have said and done both on and off the pitch. All the writing found within these pages seeks to expand our collective understanding of these individuals, moving the conversation beyond the cult of celebrity in order to examine how their individual experiences have helped to inform the complexity, integrity and multiplicity of Black life.

In some cases, the contributed essay will be based on an interview; in others, the writing will take the form of a composite of things the subject has said, an idea they've represented and fragments of their interior life they've shared. This means that the writing will vary in form, tone and approach – thereby allowing each chronologically ordered essay to offer a previously unexplored perspective.

All the writers featured in *A New Formation* have been commissioned along lines of relatability. To better understand why I felt it important to do this, it's useful to lean on the words of Linda Tuhiwai Smith, a Māori professor of Indigenous education: 'when indigenous peoples become the researchers and not merely the researched, the activity of research is transformed. Questions are framed differently, priorities are ranked differently, problems are defined differently, people participate on different terms.'[1] Smith's comments related to the Māori community from which she's drawn, but something similar can be said about what happens when Black people become the researchers. Given the abundance of joy, pride and affirmation Black players bring to football – and by extension the lives of all manner of football fans – it's strange to witness how little of that feeling is captured across the newspaper interviews and books that commonly depict their lives. *A New Formation* will work to remedy this.

Now, I know I said that this book wasn't about racism, but before we can begin the work of tying Blackness to community and kinship and heritage and home, we need to track the winding paths that Black and mixed-race players have walked that have taken them from steeling themselves in preparation for abuse to becoming leaders at the forefront of politics, all while simultaneously influencing Black British identity. To do this, we have to start at the point in history where the effects of their presence in the national game began to be felt.

The Dark Old Days

Those of us fortunate enough to have avoided the 'dark old days' of English football in the 1970s and 1980s understand them only in abstract. Even the very name – *dark old days* – lends the era the feel of mythology, as if we're to believe that it's a long-forgotten time with little bearing on the present. In order to trace our hands over the abrasive contours of this period in history, we rely on recollections relayed by family and friends or recorded in literature and documentaries. While many of these accounts detail how racial and political violence manifested on the terraces and outside stadiums – affecting both Black footballers *and* Black supporters – analyses of how this violence was combatted by law are rare.

Absolutely nothing legislative was done to check the rise of racism in football* in the 1970s. If anything, it was indirectly

* Although in this piece of writing, I am specifically seeking to understand how racism in football was legislatively addressed, it is important to recognise that, during the timeframe I am focusing on here, women's professional football in England was still banned (and efforts to rescind this ban were being thwarted by the FA). This sexist and misogynistic action – and how it affected Black women specifically – will be discussed elsewhere in *A New Formation*. LGBTQ+ football fans and players were also victims of abuse during this era; their experiences will also be explored elsewhere in the book. See page 35 for Musa Okwonga's essay on Justin Fashanu.

encouraged: in 1978, then-Conservative leader and future prime minister Margaret Thatcher validated and enabled the spread of racism in football. Speaking to current affairs programme *World in Action*, she claimed that 'People are really rather afraid that this country might be rather swamped by people with a different culture ... if there is any fear that it might be swamped, people are going to react and be rather hostile to those coming in.' These comments, read alongside Black footballers' increased participation in association football, sound tailor-made to incite racial abuse towards Black footballers and fans. By the mid-1980s, however, three significant hooligan-instigated incidents – in Luton, Birmingham and Heysel* – pushed the Home Office to commission the judge-led Popplewell Inquiry, which recommended that 'consideration should be given to creating a specific offence of chanting obscene or racialist abuse at a sports ground'.[2]

It is now unambiguously understood that Liverpool fans were in no way responsible for the Hillsborough disaster, and that the main cause was criminally incompetent policing. However, the contemporary inquiry into the tragedy, led by

* The 1985 Luton riot occurred before, during and after the 1984–85 season FA Cup sixth-round match between Luton and Millwall at Luton's Kenilworth Road ground. A mass of Millwall supporters damaged the surrounding area and large sections of the stadium. The incident of hooliganism at Birmingham City's St Andrew's Stadium took place when Birmingham-based hooligans – known as the Zulu Warriors – clashed with Leeds supporters before a 1985 league match. In the ensuing violence, a section of a wall collapsed, killing fifteen-year-old Leeds fan, Ian Hambridge. The Heysel Stadium disaster, meanwhile, was a human stampede that occurred on 29 May 1985 before the start of the 1985 European Cup Final between Juventus and Liverpool. A group of mostly Juventus fans, who were escaping from Liverpool fans who had breached an inadequately policed fence, were crushed against a wall that subsequently collapsed in the stadium in Brussels. Thirty-nine people were killed and 600 were injured in the confrontation. As a result, all English clubs were banned from the European competition for five years (Liverpool were banned for six).

Lord Justice Taylor, followed the line of thinking established in the Popplewell report by supporting the criminalisation of racist chants at football matches: 'If there is a ... specific offence of chanting obscene or racial abuse ... hooligans will know precisely what is prohibited and that they do those things at their peril.' This ideology influenced the Football (Offences) Act of 1991, which made it an 'offence to take part at a designated football match in chanting of an indecent or racialist nature'.[3]

Although it would be clumsy to suggest that the fall in the incidence of monkey chanting and other forms of racist taunting at football matches was a direct consequence of efforts to combat hooliganism, the Popplewell Inquiry's findings seem to have been a conclusive factor in its steady decline. But an unintended consequence of this research and subsequent legislative changes was the production of the stereotypical bald, badly tattooed, beer-bellied 'racist hooligan' figure, who, once identified as a moral outcast, could be publicly shamed and pronounced as antithetical to the kind of individual welcome in English football stadiums. This fixation on the obviously racist hooligan obscured the more nuanced and complex forms of racist expression that permeated British football.

At the onset of the 1990s, several factors – some soft and therefore harder to measure – converged to significantly reduce the white barbarism that had blighted the game for decades: the – highly contingent and localised – acceptance of Black spectators at certain football grounds, the modernisation of stadiums (including the widespread installation of CCTV, which is the main reason in-ground violence barely exists any more) and, of course, the irresistible and sustained presence of Black players on the pitch, who stood at the vanguard of all of these changes. More broadly, in wider society, there was an increasing move towards the concept of 'tolerance', as the seeds of multiculturalism sown in the 1970s and 1980s began to take hold. As a result, when the Let's Kick Racism Out of Football campaign – which featured Les Ferdinand and Eric Cantona (who took his role in kicking racism out of football very seriously at Selhurst Park on 25 January 1995) – was launched by the Commission for Racial Equality and the Professional Footballers' Association at the start of the 1993–94 football season, fans and clubs alike were more responsive to its mission than they probably would have been a decade earlier. Over the next four years, the organisation, which is now called Kick It Out, also secured financial backing from the FA, the Premier League and the Football Foundation to continue its anti-racism mission.*

In the era before these efforts – the aforementioned 'dark old days' – the Black footballers drip-fed into the game by intrepid and pragmatic managers were largely defenceless in the face of the sustained and merciless racist abuse they were subjected to by white supporters on a weekly basis. The only acceptable form of resistance against this sustained aggression was to endure, persist and not just win, but win well. Many of these Black players refused to be driven out of football (although the number of gifted players who were discouraged from pursuing their dreams cannot be underestimated), just as the wider African diasporic† population of the UK remained unwilling to be intimidated by fascist organisations and a

* Incredibly, it wasn't until 1997 that the Football Task Force, a national organisation that was established by Tony Blair's newly elected Labour Party to honour an election promise, recommended that anti-racism pledges be written into players' and coaches' contracts, that football clubs develop equal opportunity policies, and that referees should be directed to make racial abuse a red-card offence.

† The African diaspora refers to the vast community of people dispersed from the continent of Africa.

largely unwelcoming society that steadfastly refused to treat them as equals. Their defiant attitudes and actions – though not recognised as such at the time outside the African diasporic community – carried deep political implications that have retrospectively come to be acknowledged and appreciated by wider British society. However, at the time, these actions did not carry the same global ramifications and wider cultural impact as those of their African-American counterparts, such as the track and field athletes John Carlos and Tommie Smith's Black Power salutes on the podium at the 1968 Olympics.

For fear of ruination at the hands of the press and supporters (of both their own and rival teams), the response of Black British footballers to endless racist vitriol was often characterised by extreme restraint – the now-immortalised image of John Barnes seemingly nonchalantly back-heeling a single banana from the pitch lives on as an eternal example of this attitude. But, on occasion, their aspirations to redefine the conditions they competed under became more overt, such as in December 1974, when Leyton Orient players Laurie Cunningham and Bobby Fisher raised their fists in homage to Carlos and Smith at the Den, Millwall's home ground.

The legacy of the Black British footballer – and athlete – is one of fortitude, self-control and determination. White sports writers have attempted to construct a historical corrective for the moral failings of their era, including – although never stated explicitly – the complicity of those paid to document the spectacle of their suffering. Cyrille Regis, Laurie Cunningham, Brendon Batson, Ces Podd, Garth Crooks, John Barnes and others now populate a pantheon of near-sanctified heroes, forced to bear the burden of the white man's past sins and consequently redeem him through their strength and resilience – a narrative that overlooks the fact that, had these men dared to critique football's governing bodies for failing to protect them, they would undoubtedly have been fined, banned and censured in the press.

This rewriting of the *meaning* of Black British footballers' experiences of racist abuse is not without precedent. In his ground-breaking book *The Black Atlantic*, historian and Arsenal fan Paul Gilroy states:

> This idea of a special redemptive power produced through suffering has its ready counterpart in the writings of black thinkers who have, at various times, identified similar relationships between the history of modern racial slavery and the redemption of both Africa and America. The capacity of Blacks to redeem and transform the modern world through the truth and clarity of perception that emerge from their pain is, for example, a familiar element in the theology of Martin Luther King, Jr, which argues not only that black suffering has a meaning but that its meaning could be externalised and amplified so that it could be of benefit to the moral status of the whole world.[4]

This framing of Black suffering – the widely shared and hugely popular image of Black personal trainer and author, Patrick Hutchinson, carrying a fascist thug to safety during the BLM protests of 2020 is a contemporary example of this framing – and the propagation of the concept of Black exceptionalism* through the uncritical idealisation of Black

* Black exceptionalism is the idea that articulate, successful Black people are the exception to the rule. Black exceptionalism also holds that, in order to be worthy of documentation or any form of recognition, Black people have to be outstanding. The myth of Black exceptionalism denies Black people the ability to make mistakes and be flawed.

'firsts', underpins wider society's collective reading of these footballers. That's not to say that these players *weren't* truly outstanding and inspiring – especially to the generation of footballers who followed them (Andrew Cole, for example, cites Regis as his idol, as I'll discuss in a later chapter). But the story of the first generation of Black footballers gaining access to league sides and the England squad exemplifies first and foremost that Black players had to far outstrip their white counterparts in every conceivable way just to be considered as equal to them. Their being the 'first' anything speaks less to their innate extraordinariness and more to the fact that the institutions they entered were built on, and attempted to maintain, fundamentally racist hegemonic structures.*

The football media of the time was almost completely silent on racism. During a game between Holland and England in 1988, beloved BBC commentator John Motson described unambiguous monkey chanting directed at Dutch midfielder Ruud Gullit as 'good natured barracking'. During the Merseyside Derby that same year, the ceaseless abuse that John Barnes received, including the chants 'Everton is white' and 'Niggerpool, Niggerpool', could be heard live on the BBC but went unremarked on. This silence wasn't confined solely to the state broadcaster; rather, it was a grim reflection of the moral ineptitude of the industry and much of white society more generally.

But, as Chinua Achebe famously stated, 'The times in which we live influence our behaviour, but the best, normally the better among us ... are never held hostage by the times.'[5]

* This also applies every time a Black individual is heralded for entering a profession, playing a long-established character or winning an award for the first time.

When drawing parallels between the present day and the recent past, the role that writers and broadcasters played – or perhaps didn't play – in responding to the racism that disfigured British stadiums in the 1970s and 1980s merits careful consideration. Today, when racist incidents occur, sports desks are universally aghast. However, amid the pearl clutching and performative condemnation, there endures a collective inability on the part of many white football writers to reflect on the interrelation between obvious forms of anti-Black racism – like monkey chanting – and the fact that they have rarely, if ever, had a Black colleague or editor.

In *Pitch Black*, a thoroughly researched book about Black British footballers from the 1970s onwards, Emy Onuora suggests that:

> The unwillingness of the media generally to address in any great depth the endemic racism of football's past may reflect an unwillingness to acknowledge the role they played in contributing to the culture within football at the time ... In discussions of historic racist incidents, the blame is firmly placed at the feet of fans. With the examples of terrace behaviour cited, this conveniently ignores the media's complicity.[6]

Football media's sustained focus on painting racist football fans as uneducated, working-class and/or foreign caricatures, while simultaneously burnishing the reputations of now-retired Black footballers (while – until recently – tacitly denying them a platform to speak and write) who excelled while having bananas, phlegm and insults hurled at them, enables British society to avoid asking substantive questions about why overt mass anti-Black racism endured in the UK for decades and is now habitually attributed to a suspiciously large 'small minority'. Only when this question is confronted, and attempts are made to answer it, will we see larger numbers of Black people in positions of authority in the football industry.

By 1999, twenty per cent of professional players in English football leagues were drawn from the African diasporic community.[7] Many of these players were children of the Windrush generation, and while their growing prominence was a contributing factor in the decline of anti-Black racism in Premier League safe-seater stadiums, their hyper-visibility also resulted in a more nebulous and influential form of mistreatment that was harder to police. Through media coverage, Black footballers were habitually diminished in subtle and overt ways by former professionals (many of whom retain racist attitudes) turned pundits and columnists and journalists drawn from the white upper-middle class, who continue to arbitrate on footballing morality despite their inability to appreciate or understand cultural differences.

Of course, all footballers find their actions policed and critiqued in direct proportion to the amount they earn. However, Black footballers, like all Black citizens in the media spotlight and wider society, find themselves uniquely judged according to a matrix of moral and behavioural standards that are impossible to meet. When Black players fell foul of these ludicrously exacting requirements, they risked excoriation in the press. This threat of negative coverage had three clear effects: firstly, and perhaps most importantly, it instructed Black footballers to maintain a defensive and apolitical position, which forced them to keep their private selves and public selves separate. Secondly, this disconnecting process wrapped Black footballers in a gauzy film of inauthenticity, obscuring their experiences before presenting them to a deeply tribalistic audience already disinclined to like them. Finally, it led to the construction of one-dimensional narratives (the outspoken critic of 'racism in football', the cage footballer from the single-parent household, the player only saved from prison by football),[8] which the press then paternalistically demanded the Black footballer to entrench without acknowledging their role in the creation of these narratives.

A 'ground-breaking'[9] 2020 report by Danish research firm RunRepeat confirmed what members of the African diasporic community have protested since time immemorial: Black players are likely to be recognised for their physicality and athleticism, whereas white players are lauded for their intelligence, technical quality and work ethic. This tendency is a stressor that contributes to racial weathering,[*] and although increasingly obvious to all but the most belligerently racist football fan, feels familiar. However, there are also countless examples of the British media subtly drawing into question the *attitudes* of Black players, othering them through character assassination or mockery: Carlton Palmer[†] as an enduring punchline; the suspicion that John Barnes's indifferent form for England could be attributed to his Jamaican heritage; 'comedian' David Baddiel repeatedly

* The weathering hypothesis was first proposed by Arline Geronimus in 1992. It posits that health issues experienced by African-American women are precipitated and exacerbated by socioeconomic stressors. Here I am expanding its usage to include the psychological impact that racially coded language has on Black footballers and Black football fans.

† For younger readers, Carlton Palmer is a retired England international who played for several English league clubs but is most widely associated with Sheffield Wednesday. Due to his ungainly playing style he invited an undue amount of mockery from the football media and opposition fans.

'blacking up', placing a pineapple on his head and acting as if he were dimwitted to impersonate former Nottingham Forest player Jason Lee on national television; 'Cashley' Cole; the sustained efforts to dismantle Rio Ferdinand's credibility after *that* missed drugs test; and the perpetual, press-led victimisation of Raheem Sterling.

Analysing the 'psychosis of whiteness'* is an exercise that Black studies academic Kehinde Andrews likened to venturing 'into a house of mirrors'.[10] While this is certainly true, it would be remiss of me not to elaborate on why the aforementioned behaviours continue to menace Black footballers, and from where they might stem.

Racial Insularity and a Lack of Imagination

Throughout history, people of the African diaspora who live in predominantly white societies have been required to understand their hosts incredibly well to ensure their literal and economic survival. In her essay 'What's missing from *White Fragility*', the American culture critic Lauren Michele Jackson cites two examples of this enduring phenomenon:

> As the Ex-Colored Man claims in the 1912 novel [*The Autobiography of an Ex-Coloured Man]* by James Weldon Johnson, 'the colored people of this country know and understand the white people better than the white people

* In critical race studies whiteness is understood as a social process that can, according to Andrews, induce a form of psychosis in white people identified by traits such irrationality, denial and a superiority complex which are beyond any rational engagement.

know and understand them.' Or, as [W E B] Du Bois eerily conveys in his 1920 essay 'The souls of white folk': 'Of them I am singularly clairvoyant. I see in and through them ... I see these souls undressed and from the back and side. I see the working of their entrails. I know their thoughts and they know that I know.'[11]

Perhaps the most popular summation of this tendency was articulated by James Baldwin, who in *Remember This House* – an unfinished work of nonfiction that formed the basis of the 2016 documentary *I Am Not Your Negro* – proclaimed: 'You give me a terrifying advantage. You never had to look at me. I had to look at you. I know more about you than you know about me.'

While there is no formal manual passed down between generations of Black families, their collective study of white cultural norms works as an oral tradition, comprising anecdotes, warnings and dark caustic humour,* which serves to inform, protect and bind. However, as Baldwin emphasises, this study is not reciprocal.†

The unidirectional nature of this dynamic was candidly and unwittingly illustrated by Matt Hughes, then-deputy football correspondent for *The Times*, no less than a week after Raheem Sterling was racially abused by Chelsea supporter Colin Wing

* Excerpts from this oral tradition include, but are by no means limited to: Black parents teaching their children how to keep police officers calm; the knowledge that a large proportion of the British population would, if pressed, choose the life of a dog over that of a refugee; and the collective understanding that white people steadfastly refuse to wash or adequately season their chicken.

† Although Baldwin was specifically addressing white America, the conditions that Black writers address across the Atlantic often have analogues in British society.

in 2018. His contribution to the discourse engendered by the incident, unironically headlined 'Racism would be far worse without football', found him reflecting on his social milieu:

> Halfway through a week of reflection triggered by the alleged racist abuse of Raheem Sterling and his brave response in calling out perceived racism in the media came a shocking realisation: of the hundreds of numbers in my phone, the only ones belonging to black people were those of individuals working in football. Despite living and working in one of the most cosmopolitan cities in the world ... my social and professional circle is 'hideously white'.[12]

Despite this new-found and profoundly moving self-knowledge, Hughes lacked the insight to address a paradox inherent in the spectacle of football that sociologist Ben Carrington identified in his book *Race, Sport and Politics*: 'The sports field is often the space where we are most likely to find forms of fanatical hyper-identification and even idolised devotion towards black athletic bodies *and* some of the most violent expressions of anti-black racism, sometimes occurring within the same sporting locations and directed towards the *very* same athletes.'[13] Carrington's analysis doesn't entirely explode Hughes's almost child-like assumption that the presence of Black people in football improves the state of 'race relations' in Britain, but it does add a layer of complexity that a great many white football writers, by dint of their identities and experiences, simply fail to consider.

Hughes's piece was met with ridicule on Black Twitter for a level of self-awareness more commonly associated with cringeworthy *The Office* character David Brent – but it should be noted that Hughes is one of the only writers in the hyper-white world of football writing* to even attempt such broad and personal self-analysis.† Furthermore, it is important to outline the relevance of a disclosure like Hughes's to the representation of football in British society, and, more specifically, to portrayals of Black footballers, who are required to seem relatable but are simultaneously distanced from the public as a direct result of white media hegemony.

Perhaps the most devastating consequence of this is the restriction of the Black experience in football – which, as this book will show through its varied contributors, is abundant – to something that can be examined only through its relationship to racism. This systemic reductivism persists, perhaps conversely, because many white football writers are far more comfortable asking for insights on this topic from Black footballers than from white players – or indeed from themselves. The (white) writer and the Black footballer sit down in mutual agreement that racism is *bad* and, although the Black footballer may not

* According to the Black Collective of Media in Sports, just two of the fifty-one sports journalists sent by British newspapers to Euro 2016 were drawn from the global majority; no mainstream British newspaper has ever had a Black sports editor; there are no Black sports columnists at any of the national mainstream papers (and any previous Black columnists have all been current or former professional sportspeople, rather than sports journalists); only six of 456 roles across broadcast and written media covering Wimbledon 2016, Euro 2016 and the 2016 Olympics and Paralympics were filled by BAME women; and, similarly, only eight of the 456 roles covering summer events in 2016 went to Black journalists who had not played sport professionally. Journalists are less ethnically diverse than the workforce as a whole. According to 2017 data from the National Council for the Training of Journalists, just one per cent of UK journalists are Black. Meanwhile, in a 2016 survey of British journalists by the Reuters Institute, Black Britons made up just 0.2 per cent of the sample despite accounting for approximately three per cent of the British population.

† Although it was probably not intentional, Hughes also revealed the racial insularity of white Britain that Black British people long suspected but were unable to explicitly corroborate.

open up *significantly* about the depressingly common eventuality of facing racism, they will regurgitate a usable soundbite that slots readily into a preordained storyline.

Black studies scholar Christina Sharpe explains why this process is so durable. In a talk titled 'Still Here', she critiques a review by a white author that crucially misunderstood – and undermined – the attempts of a group of Black writers to speak about a specific area of concern in their lives:

> What we encounter then, in this writing, is a deficit of imagination on the part of *that* writer, which is indicative of the way that, [what] for lack of a better term I will call the 'white imagination' determines and misreads ... We cannot afford to be hailed by that misreading and called into being by that deficit – that deficit is not of *our* imagining.[14]

The combination of the 'racial insularity' exemplified by Matt Hughes and Sharpe's theory of the 'white imagination' (and the deficit it can't help but conjure) is a useful way to frame and understand the inability of the mainstream football media to contextualise Black individuality in any meaningful depth.

Yet, despite these systemic obstructions, any and all attempts to distance Black footballers from the wider African diasporic community in the UK are doomed to failure. The football industry remains one of the few arenas in which Black people can bear witness to the sustained or sporadic triumphs of people who look and sound like them. This affiliation is rooted in the knowledge that Black people have partly tracked their shifting position in British society through the motions of Black footballers – moving in lockstep, quietly mapping their identities onto men and women whose origins, experiences and aspirations continue to reflect their own.

The highest echelons of the football industry remain hermetically sealed off from the average football fan, the associated economic disparities too vast to allow for any profound connection with the players who populate it. For Black supporters, however, thanks to an innate historical and cultural overlap, Black players resemble members of an extended family. In Hope Powell they see the stoicism and quiet aspiration embodied by their parents' generation. The tribulations of Ravel Morrison bring to mind a cousin whose creases couldn't be ironed out. Ian Wright could be the enduringly cool uncle, Anita Asante could be Grandma's favourite grandchild. Inextricably linked with this identification is a recognition that Black footballers, on behalf of Black people, have created leg room under the table, created new customs and forced our features into the nation's family portrait.

Transformation and Liberation

The only recourse available to the Black footballer of the seventies was to 'let their football do the talking' (a sadly persistent and idiotic maxim that suggests goals and assists can do the work of anti-racism) or adopt a role that conformed to, rather than confronted, the status quo. Thanks to a shifting social and cultural climate, the reality of today's Black footballers feels drastically different. An increasing range of Black public figures are rigorously challenging the obligation to be spokespeople for a problem not of their making, and – by extension – critiquing the monoculturalism of the industries that push them to do so.

In a series of tweets in January 2020, author Reni Eddo-Lodge revealed that she had gone as far as to change her contact details so that producers and researchers could no longer ask her to take part in 'debates' whose primary function was to drive ratings and social media engagement. 'The question of how to discuss anti-racism with the widest possible audience is never going to be answered by a television producer named Poppy working at ITV studios,' she tweeted. While Eddo-Lodge was careful not to cast aspersions on those who choose to approach the metaphorical podium, journalist and co-founder of Black lifestyle platform *Black Ballad*, Tobi Oredein, went a step further. 'Praising someone who sits on debate shows for a cheque to debate their humanity and then writes a column isn't going to solve our problems. It brings nothing but individual praise and a superficial diversity chat,' she tweeted.

This pushback, and the reasoning behind it, was introduced to a football audience by Ian Wright. While working as a pundit for the BBC before the 2019 FA Cup Final between Raheem Sterling's Manchester City and Watford, Wright was invited by Gary Lineker to discuss whether speaking out against racism, as Sterling had done repeatedly, was 'brave'. Rather than stick to the script and dutifully confirm that, yes, it was indeed 'brave' to ask white society to view you as a human being, Wright took a left turn, and used the fifty seconds afforded to him to make a broader point about the terms on which these conversations rest:

> What 'appens is, if you come out and just start talking about it, people kinda shut that down, because they say 'Oh, here we go again, playing the race card' . . . It always seems to happen, Gal, when there's an incident, and then, all of a sudden, *then* you *can* speak, and then you see them trotting out people for three to four minutes on the television, on shows, trying to explain the complexity of racism. It's very complex – it's

something that cannot be dealt with by somebody saying 'Ah, let's get Ian Wright for three minutes, let's get John Barnes on for three minutes.' It's not gonna work like that.

Wright's frustration with the failure of the commentariat to sincerely engage with anti-racism was palpable, and he was not alone in feeling this way. In October 2019, the day after the Black contingent of the England men's national team were greeted by the familiar sound of monkey chanting and unashamed Sieg Heil salutes as they took on Bulgaria at the Vasil Levski National Stadium, a succession of Black and mixed-raced former footballers revealed they had been contacted by radio and television producers to validate the mood of performative solemnity this incident gave rise to in white Britain. However, to avoid being asked to relive experiences of similar abuse or being hurriedly pressed for a manifesto to solve the 'problem' of 'racism in football', they declined the invites en masse.

First, pundit and broadcaster Stan Collymore shared a screenshot of a generic email sent to his management by *Good Morning Britain* with the caption 'No thanks @GMB, my race isn't a 2 min bit before you give someone from *Geordie Shore* an hour to show you their new nails.' Next, in a now-deleted tweet, former Sheffield United midfielder and current manager of Gainsborough Trinity Curtis Woodhouse responded, 'Big fan of the show ... but I agree with what @StanCollymore and @IanWright0 said. I won't be churned out for 3 minutes to discuss this issue. I'm not here to dance,' to a request from a BBC Radio Humberside producer. Eniola Aluko struck preemptively, declaring via tweet, 'I won't be coming on any shows today to state the obvious ... Stop talking/distracting/delaying, start changing and doing.'

Mirroring these refusals, Les Ferdinand – at the time of writing the only Black technical director in English football – revealed in an official QPR club statement in September 2020, that he was no longer coming to the table to talk about racism. 'Recently, I took the decision not to do any more interviews on racism in football because the debate was going around in circles,' Ferdinand said. 'People want a nice soundbite when something happens, but how many of the media ... genuinely want change?'[15] This position marks a profound transformation in the way Black consciousness is willing to engage with a socio-political environment that has sought to constrain and control it for so long.

The late Toni Morrison famously described racism as a 'distraction' that keeps those who experience it from doing the 'work' – that is, from finding their purpose in life. She also understood that racism was a problem that white people urgently needed to confront. In an appearance on *The Charlie Rose Show* in 1993, and with unblinking acuity, she explained to Rose that, as a child, she realised that white Americans were emotionally bereft and morally inferior to the Black citizens they victimised. This neurotic need to inflict, Morrison elaborated, made those who participated 'feel good', and that was its service to them. If it were ever removed, they would need to ask serious questions about the validity of their lives and identities after that point. 'I take your race away,' Morrison said, 'and there you are, all strung out and all you got is your lil' self. And what is that? What are you without racism? Are you any good? Are you still strong? Are you still smart? Do you still like yourself? These are the questions.' Morrison made it clear that she need not be involved in the subsequent actions or dialogue required to end it: 'My feeling is, white people have a very, very serious problem, and they should start thinking about what they can do about it. Take *me* out of it.'

Lilian Thuram echoed these points in September 2019, a few days after Belgium and Inter Milan striker Romelu Lukaku was abused by Cagliari fans – yet another incident to add to the miasma of racial intolerance that Italian society fosters with such alacrity:

> We must realise that the world of football is not racist, but rather that there is racism in Italian culture, French culture, European culture and more generally in white culture. We must have the courage to say that white people think they are superior and believe that they are ... if they consider themselves more important and express that with monkey noises, it means they have an inferiority complex. It is up to them to find a solution to their problem.[16]

After retiring in 2008, Thuram, a world-class defender who played with distinction for Parma, Juventus and Barcelona while also amassing more international caps for France than anyone else in the country's history, became a committed anti-racism campaigner. (Although, in truth, his incursions into the political landscape began in 2005 when he rebuked then-French president, Nicolas Sarkozy, for referring to poor, young Black people and other people of colour who don't fall into the 'Black exceptionalism' narrative as 'racaille', or 'scum'.) Thuram's anti-racism activities also extended to the curation of an exhibition held at the Musée du quai Branly in Paris, titled *Human Zoos: The Invention of the Savage*, which examined the use of colonial subjects in zoos and freak shows. In both intent and practice, Thuram's efforts are as principled an example of anti-racism work that you could hope to find. Yet he too has known for quite some time that the responsibility of this labour should not rest upon his, nor any other Black person's shoulders.

Similarly, during an interview recorded for the COPA90 documentary *Beat the Bias*, former Manchester City and England defender Micah Richards posed an increasingly common rhetorical question: 'Who invented racism? It wasn't Black people, so why should we be the ones to solve it?"'* While the communion of perspectives shared by Morrison, Thuram and Richards can be analysed through a lens that takes into account social interactions between Black people – W E B Du Bois understood parallels in global Black thought and expressive culture as the result of 'one long memory' – it is also the consequence of the observational power that Black people have been forced to develop in order to rationalise the behaviours of white people.

An acknowledgement that the onus to combat racism is on white people, with a subsequent transferral of this responsibility, represents the first and most important step in the arduous journey towards the psychological emancipation – from the twin tasks of battling racism and navigating the imagined anxieties of white people – that African diasporic people seek. In recent history, achieving even this initial step felt impossible. But with their actions guided by the explicitly politicised position they have assumed, Black footballers are helping to nudge this objective out of the realm of possibility and into that of reality. Their ability to initiate this profound shift is in large part rooted in football's potency – more specifically in how they have leveraged its seismic influencing power.

Understanding football solely as a 'game' is akin to believing that the purpose of sex is procreation, or that food is only fuel. Football is far more than a spectacle confined to a pitch: the events that take place on the field offer moments of

* Reader, I co-directed this documentary. I asked Micah if he felt that Black players should be operating as anti-racism campaigners within the game and these were the questions he *immediately* shot back.

pure transcendence and provide the lifeblood of lifelong friendships. Football is unique in its universality, in its capacity to bind families and nations – albeit temporarily – while being simultaneously ridiculous, funny and eminently memeable. Perhaps most importantly, only religion can rival football in terms of inspiring people's fanatical devotion. With all that considered, football's power to influence the cultural landscape and dramatically shift mindsets should not be underestimated.

A Change Is Coming

Adopting an anti-racist political position – and thereby taking on the weight of the right-leaning media contingent – remains a dangerous choice for Black athletes. In an extract from his book *Full Dissidence: Notes From an Uneven Playing Field*, ESPN columnist Howard Bryant details that those who take a stand 'would become outcasts, active enemies within their industries, weakening their job prospects and endorsement opportunities, increasing the daily stress in jobs that are competitive and difficult enough as it is'. Bryant continues: 'They become *problems.* Or they will be ignored by the industry friends and teammates they thought they had. All of this is the human cost of supporting blackness, even in the heavily integrated industry of professional sports.'[17] While Bryant is referring to the experiences of African-American athletes, who contend with a far more overtly racist media glare and political reality, it is unlikely that Black British footballers would have escaped similar consequences had they taken similar action. As Sara Ahmed observes in her brilliant book *Living a Feminist Life*, 'When you expose a problem you pose a problem.'[18]

Following this logic, Raheem Sterling's decision, in December 2018, to carefully critique the print and online press – who'd spent the past three years victimising him – should have resulted in waves of familiar hostility that no amount of wealth or superlative form could have shielded him from. So it was astonishing that his statement had the opposite effect. As a direct consequence of it, high-profile members of the broadcast media began, at long last, to reckon with their individual failure to stand with Black footballers in the various capacities in which they had previously interacted with them (although it should be noted that the *Daily Mail* and *The Sun*, at the very least, seemingly remain committed to their standard nefarious behaviour).

The day after Sterling spoke out, Gary Neville revealed on Sky Sports's *Monday Night Football* that, when he was England coach, Sterling – distressed at the treatment meted out to him by the media – had come to see him a few days before the team's disastrous exit from Euro 2016. Neville had attempted to minimise the problem:

> I told him he was a great player and we loved him to bits ... and tried to almost patch him up to get him to a point where he can play without addressing the underlying issue. But on reflection now that may have been brushing it aside a little bit in all honesty.

Neville then contrasted the excuses made for Harry Kane's risible performances with the personal language used to attack Sterling:

> Harry Kane, who is the blue-eyed boy of English football ... was having a difficult time in that tournament and it was portrayed that it was because he was on corners. Raheem was having a difficult time and it was portrayed as other reasons, more personal reasons at times, and the language

> used towards him was difficult ... the abuse he received, particularly in the media, beyond that tournament, and the language that was used, was something I've not seen before.

Neville is arguably the most insightful and socially conscious white pundit* currently operating, and can often be found drawing parallels between the anti-immigration rhetoric that powers the Conservative Party and isolated incidents of racial abuse in football. Later on in the programme, Neville also elaborated on the fact that, no matter how successful a Black footballer becomes, the adulation received by white players eludes them:

> Over the last few days, I have heard people say 'Gazza got stick and David Beckham got stick and Wayne Rooney got stick' ... Gazza was hero-worshipped when it was good. Becks was hero-worshipped when it was good. It was unbelievable for those lads. They were up here. So you are missing the point to say they got stick when it was bad, because when Ashley Cole and Raheem Sterling are up there [Neville extends his hand far above his head] it doesn't get that good, they don't get the appreciation.

Turning his attention to England's resistance to modifying its national identity in ways that might finally include Black people, and to the systematic gaslighting that Black footballers have endured for over seventy years, Neville continued:

> I even look back to my time coaching with England when Rickie Lambert scored that goal or when Jamie Vardy came into the team – 'Oh, he is one of ours.' But it wasn't like that

* Competition for this role is non-existent.

> when Danny Welbeck came in, or when Marcus Rashford came into the squad ... The evidence is actually quite heavy when you start to look at it in terms of the appreciation of the Black players compared to the white players that played for England.

Neville's words were without precedent in mainstream British football broadcasting. As if to emphasise the tone of honesty and accountability that underscored his assessment, he admitted that he too was 'part of the problem'. That same day, talkSPORT radio host Adrian Durham built on Neville's moment of near-nigrescence* with an impassioned, pre-written statement the likes of which his employer had not aired before (it was not until a year later that Hugh Woozencroft became the station's first Black host). In the seven-minute proclamation, Durham made clear-sighted points seemingly at odds with the imagined white-van man talkSPORT audience:

> The racist agenda is clear, and it's sad that some who have huge and influential voices and big platforms in this country cannot see it ... I've spoken about the racist agenda against Sterling in the past and it's been dismissed, mainly by white men. And that's what you'll have seen since Saturday evening as well – white men claiming that the fan at Chelsea said 'Manc', not 'Black'. Well, they're tryna twist the truth for a reason: the first step for any racist is to deny that racism exists.

* Nigrescence describes a process of becoming Black or developing a racial identity. The term was popularised by William E Cross Jr, who included a theory of nigrescence in his ground-breaking 1991 book *Shades of Black: Diversity in African American Identity* (Philadelphia, PA: Temple University Press).

Crucially, an increasingly exasperated Durham then made the connection that, though not necessarily *denied* by many well-meaning white people, had never been directly acknowledged: 'Every one of us in the media has a duty. We're tryna change what's been happening for centuries – slavery, apartheid, the Ku Klux Klan, the murder of Stephen Lawrence, monkey chants and bananas.' In so doing, he exploded the comfortable concept that racism is a sequence of seemingly unrelated random acts rather than the inevitable manifestations of a deeply bigoted culture that has been nurtured over hundreds of years. By the end of the statement, he was channelling his inner James Baldwin: 'By attempting to dehumanise them, you're actually dehumanising yourself. Look at yourself and what you've become.'

Whether Neville or Durham would have felt moved to speak were it not for the influence of Sterling's statement is open to debate. Regardless, when both men spoke publicly in 2018, they formed a band of outriders howling into the wind of denial and whataboutery that statements such as theirs tend to attract.

Nearly two years later, the global Black Lives Matter protests of June 2020 – a historic moment during which even the legendary American political activist Angela Davis felt buoyed by hope and optimism – tilted the world's axis and added jet fuel to the 'racism in football' discourse. In short, the public execution of George Floyd by the Minneapolis Police Department, during a period when national lockdowns made it far harder to ignore, indirectly spurred a broader coalition of white voices in the football industry to finally join the fray rather than stand quietly to the side. Jake Humphrey, the main presenter of BT Sport's football coverage, took to Instagram to let his followers know that he too 'had to do better' – whatever that means – while, live on Sky Sports, full-time-Paul-Pogba-critic Graeme Souness desperately pleaded with his fellow pundit Micah Richards to teach him how to be a better anti-racist.

These conversations – which, at the time of writing, have been confined to social media and TV studios – have not yet brought about institutional change, nor are they bound to the broader political aims of Black liberation. But they *have* indisputably helped to increase the cache of power that Black footballers already hold (thanks in large part to social media, which allows them to say what they want, when they want to, to huge audiences). There are two ways to read the current situation, and both angles are valid: we are witnessing the act of Black suffering being used as a teachable moment for the wider world, and simultaneously observing Black footballers reshaping parts of modern football in their image.

The Premier League, which had done much to purge political messaging – bar grown men dressed as poppies, that is – from its body politic, listened to Wes Morgan and Troy Deeney, the Leicester and Watford captains respectively, when they argued that 'Black Lives Matter' should replace players' names on the backs of match day kits and advocated taking a knee at the start of all league games after Project Restart.* It should be emphasised, however, that the Premier League never publicly acknowledged or attempted to explore the direct line that ran between the Black Lives Matter protests and George Floyd's public execution – which suggests that those invested in the institution are yet to develop a critical consciousness. It was, more often than not, left for the Black pundits in the studio to elaborate on that.

* Project Restart was the nickname given to the Premier League's attempts to resume the season that was interrupted by the COVID-19 pandemic on 13 March 2020.

Although Deeney and the recently retired Morgan may one day take up important administrative or technical roles in a governing body, or perhaps with their clubs, neither man represents the future *on* the pitch. But a coalition of younger players is waiting to follow their example.

Speaking to *Frieze* in 2019, the lauded African-American artist Carrie Mae Weems articulated a specific nuance of the Black experience: 'Black people are working from the position of "we". We talk about community much more. We talk about who we are as a people emerging out of a situation.'[19] Liverpool and England right-back Trent Alexander-Arnold exemplified this positionality in a discussion he had on BT Sport with Rio Ferdinand in June 2020, when he outlined that isolated incidents of racial abuse directed at Black people in society and at his colleagues affected him too. 'I feel the pain that they feel,' he said. 'It's a community feeling.' In the twenty-minute discussion – which took in subjects ranging from a lack of opportunity, institutional racism and the role that education must play in eradicating racism – Alexander-Arnold went further than any Black footballer from earlier generations would have dared, even if they wanted to. 'I wanna look back and think "I influenced a generation",' he said. 'I wanna be someone that's made a change [to] the way people think, the way the system is. If, at the end of my career, if I haven't done that I'd see that as a failure on my behalf.'

Whether Alexander-Arnold was aware that a wholehearted commitment to these comments would effectively transform his very existence into an act of ongoing political labour is unclear. And while white writers opine about the rise of the so-called 'activist-player', their excitable words perpetually fail to address the fact that the individuals who wield actual structural power, like Aleksander Čeferin, UEFA president, have made few – if any – concessions to the demands of these young up-and-comers.

Furthermore, to focus on the notion that Black players are having a political awakening would be grossly inaccurate and deeply insulting; rather, it should be understood that an overwhelmingly white football media, along with the reluctance of organisational bodies to support Black players and a social climate that accused anyone daring to protest it of 'playing the race card' previously worked to silence them. Instead, what we're witnessing is a transformation in how Black footballers are publicly engaging with the issues that affect the communities from which they're drawn. Raheem Sterling may have scythed a path through a barbarous thicket in 2018, but a choir of Black footballers' voices – both men and women – have broadened it into a fortified clearing.

None of these changes feels transient. Manchester United striker Marcus Rashford was awarded an MBE in 2020 for campaigning to end child food poverty, the following year it was revealed he donated 125 per cent of his wealth to charitable causes. Throughout the COVID-19 pandemic, Crystal Palace's Wilfried Zaha gave free accommodation to NHS nurses, Watford captain Troy Deeney's partner Alisha Hosannah designed the Black Lives Matter logo that appeared on Premier League club shirts, and the couple then licensed the logo for use, donating 100 per cent of the profits to the Stephen Lawrence Trust. Aston Villa's Tyrone Mings attended the Black Lives Matter marches, sat down to speak with UEFA to discuss racism in football and publicly challenged the Home Secretary, Priti Patel, on Twitter. Raheem Sterling has mooted a players' taskforce to combat racism in consultation with the Premier League and established his own charitable foundation.

Writing in *The Times* in 2019, Sterling expressed a sentiment uttered by peoples drawn from across the African diaspora: 'I don't want the next generation to suffer like me.'[20] As a result of his actions, and those of other Black players, future generations of Black people – including those who enter the world of professional football – may be less taxed by the onerous burden of combatting racism.

At that point, the task will be to move beyond what Keguro Macharia, a Kenyan-born professor of English and comparative literature, described in *The New Inquiry* as 'black negation'. Macharia understands this move, which remains for many a knotty concept, not as a sidestepping of obligation but as a mentally liberating exercise that decentres the negative effects of whiteness and the sometimes traumatic study of Blackness in relation to its 'lack'. 'I am uninterested,' Macharia writes, 'in remaining within the dynamics of oppression and resistance, oppression and agency, as the dominant frames within which Black life is to be thought and theorised.'[21]

Macharia, and many others within the African diaspora, are straining to break free of a worldview that will only understand or engage with their experiences so long as they orbit around the concept of an eternal struggle against racism. For this reason, even as Black footballers continue to show a willingness to juggle their careers as elite sportspeople (with all the pressure and scrutiny that invites) with functioning as spokespeople for Black liberation, it is worth pausing to consider whether this dynamic – and the narratives that are built to reify it – is fair, given the considerable psychological toll it takes on Black people to exist in this capacity, or ultimately helpful.

Relatedly, the damaging conflation of Black footballers with the racism they inevitably endure is so entrenched that little writing exists that doesn't feature one without the other.

At best, this transforms such writing into the consumption of everyone's least favourite root vegetables; at worst, for Black fans at least, it acts as an unnecessary reiteration of trauma.

Motivated by a simple refusal to accept that Black footballers – and people – can exist only as virtuous moralisers sent to teach the white world how to 'do better', as individuals who've beaten the odds presented by an anti-Black society or as wayward, money-grabbing disruptors, the assembled contributors to *A New Formation* have sought to define the players they've profiled or written about as *people*. We have done so with an acknowledgement that the journey to the point where a book like this can exist has been characterised by injustice, tragedy and loss, but it has also taken in exuberance and created a sense of Black collectivism that has lifted us up, remoulding the Black experience in the process.

Most members of the African diasporic community understand that existing beyond the grasp of anti-Black racism remains a fantastical prospect, especially in white-majority societies. But even as this fact casts a shadow over our lived realities, and as the urgent work of anti-racism in all its myriad forms continues, room must also be made for Blackness to exist beyond the confines of racism and the harmful effects of whiteness – not as a means of abrogating responsibility, but so that the multitudes that exist within Blackness can be understood and explored in their own right.

JUSTIN FASHANU

Tomorrow Never Came

Musa Okwonga

In 2017, much to the excitement of scientists, an unknown object emerged from the depths of the cosmos and cut a majestic arc across the night sky. The object, travelling too fast to be trapped by the gravitational pull of any star system, tore through our Solar System and then surged back out into the open ocean of the universe. Never before had an interstellar visitor passed through our region of space, and so, when astronomers came to name this mysterious immigrant, they called it 'Oumuamua, which roughly translates from Hawaiian as 'a messenger from afar arriving first'.

Sometimes, when I think of Justin Fashanu – the first openly gay footballer to play in the men's professional game, and still the only Black one – I think of 'Oumuamua. For, just like that ageless voyager, Fashanu was elusive, fast-moving and ultimately unknowable. Like 'Oumuamua, Fashanu was gone from each new place just as quickly as he had arrived there: in his nineteen years as a footballer, he played for twenty-two clubs, an existence not so much nomadic as frantic. Like 'Oumuamua, he bewitched every expert who observed him, soaring into the uppermost reaches of the English game with a spectacular strike against one of the finest teams in Europe. Yet Fashanu was painfully and utterly subject to the laws of footballing gravity. Instead of accelerating into the distance, untouched and undefeated, he found himself torn to the ground by overwhelming forces. By the age of thirty-seven, he was dead.

It is grim to think that the name of the first Black footballer to command a transfer fee of £1 million, a sum paid in 1981 by Nottingham Forest to take him from Norwich City, is mostly remembered as a cautionary tale – a warning that sport is no place for gay male players. Yet his demise was not inevitable. When a life implodes, as Fashanu's did, too little thought is given to the astonishing invisible pressures that are constantly exerted upon it. Too little thought is given to the choices that individuals made, or did not make, to help Fashanu when he needed them most. When I spoke with Ambrose Mendy, the sports agent who represented the ill-fated footballer for several years, he was unequivocal on this matter. 'Every professional footballer,' he told me, 'should hold their head in shame.'

By now, the facts of Fashanu's early life are fairly well known, at least in outline. He and his younger brother John, who was nineteen months his junior, were born in London. Following their parents' separation, they were placed in care by their mother since she did not have the financial means to bring them up. The brothers were then raised in Shropham in Norfolk by Alf and Betty Jackson, their white foster parents. There were very few Black people in the whole of Norfolk at the time, and the brothers were subjected to a significant degree of racial discrimination. Justin became a figure who John looked to for physical and emotional protection, and the cost of being that shield was severe. By several accounts, it made Justin acquire a mask for his emotions that he would not truly remove throughout his entire life.

Every now and then, though, Justin's face betrayed itself. *Forbidden Games*, a 2017 Netflix documentary about his life,[1] features a scene in which he was being interviewed on *Trial By Night*, a programme on regional Scottish television. A member of the audience, when asked to contribute, states that he doesn't dislike Justin because of the colour of his skin; instead, he says, 'It's his vile homosexual lifestyle that I detest.' Justin responds calmly enough (although he still appears somewhat rattled), remarking – in what is perhaps a telling slip of the tongue – that 'You don't know about my vile homophobic lifestyle.' It is striking that the audience member chose to pat himself on the back for not being racist, which also says something about the level of racism that was present at the time.

It occurs to me that there are still many people who do not know what homophobia actually is. There are people who think that it is a form of insult that can be shrugged off with sufficient resilience, allowing the target of these insults to get on with their lives and emerge stronger for their experience. But, as any gay or bisexual person will tell you, homophobia is not mere name-calling. It is a border still present in too many hearts and minds. In some environments, homophobia is the invisible tripwire in every conversation that, when triggered, can cause the ground to explode beneath you.

Aslie Pitter knows this all too well. A swift and skilful right-back, he was a gifted enough footballer to have been offered trials at Wimbledon, and to play non-league football for Carshalton and Sutton United. He was born in 1960, a year before Justin, and so his experiences are a useful yardstick for the kind of prejudice that Justin suffered. I met Aslie when, having come out as bisexual, I went to play for Stonewall FC, a London-based football club that was founded in 1991 as a place where gay and bisexual men could find community while playing the game they loved. When I arrived at Stonewall at the age of twenty-three, Aslie – though he was by then in his early forties – was still one of the fittest and quickest players at the club. As one of the older Black players, and one of the most welcoming people at Stonewall, he was a key figure in my search for self-acceptance and happiness. It was harrowing, then, to hear about one particular episode in his life.

'I was playing for a local team [composed mostly of heterosexual players],' Aslie told me, 'and I had joined Stonewall by this time. So, I was playing for Stonewall on a Sunday morning and playing with this other side on a Saturday afternoon, and I loved it. I was having fun.' At that point, he said, he had not told anyone at his local team that he was gay. 'I kind of kept my mouth shut [about my sexuality] in the early days,' he said, 'because I had this fear that they were not going to pick me, that they wouldn't want to be friends with me any more, that they wouldn't want to be around the changing rooms if I was there.' Soon enough, though, he would find himself put on the spot:

> It was the Gay Games in 1994, and [news of] it made the papers. So I told the guys from my local team that I was going off to America to play in a football tournament – and I didn't say what tournament it was, but I knew that the papers had picked up on the fact that a gay football team was going to compete at the Gay Games in New York. So, one of my teammates, who had introduced me to the club, was reading the papers and saw this. So he quizzed me at the clubhouse, in front of a load of my teammates. And he was pushing and pushing, and he was doing it quite light-heartedly – he wasn't being cruel – and he was saying, 'So, what is this tournament you're playing in in America?' And I floundered a little bit, and then I admitted, 'Well, it's the Gay Games in New York.' And so he just came out and asked me, 'Are you gay then?' And I said, 'Yes I am.' And it just went quiet.

In revealing his sexuality, Aslie had done what many might have encouraged him to do in such a situation. He was being true to himself, and being open about who he was in a straightforward manner. Yet there would be consequences for his honesty:

> At the time, I was playing for the first team for this club – they had six teams, and I was playing first team. So I completed the rest of that season, and I had a good season, I think we ended up third or fourth in the league. And then the following season, I played one game for the first team, then I got dropped. And what's supposed to happen is that if you get dropped from the first team you play for the second team, if you get dropped from the second team you play for the third team, and so on. But I got dropped from the first team, and nobody picked me up. I ended up playing for the fourth team.

Unfortunately, as Aslie observed, his fate was not much better in his new surroundings:

> The captain [of the fourth team] was a very, very aggressive, bald, big, loud, cockney guy where every second word out of his mouth was one beginning with 'c' and ending with 't'. And in this particular game – the one game I played for them – he kept calling the opposition captain, a really good player, he kept calling him – can I say the word? – he kept calling him 'pussy faggot'. So, at half-time, I said, 'Excuse me, I've got something to say,' and he says 'Yeah', and I said, 'Do you have to keep calling that guy a pussy faggot?' On that, this guy turned on me, and he said, 'Is he your fucking boyfriend? Does he fuck you up the arse?' And this guy let

> this tirade out at me, and I just stood there. No one defended me. They all stood there and watched.

This confrontation was so dispiriting that Aslie's heart wasn't in it any more:

> At the end of the game, when we all went to have a shower, I just thought, *I'm not going to have a shower.* I just changed out of the kit, threw it in the kit bag, got my tracksuit and put it on, and I went up to the manager and said, 'That was my last game,' and I walked out. And that was it. And I felt crushed, I felt tired … It's funny: when I left, nobody from the club actually phoned. It was quite a well-organised club – when people weren't around, they phoned to see how they were, and things like that – and nobody actually phoned to say, 'What's happened? Where have you been?' Nobody has said anything to this day, some twenty-eight or twenty-nine years later. Nobody has ever phoned me to find out what happened.

Watching Justin go from club to club, I wondered how often people from the places he left so rapidly would get in touch to ask after him. My suspicion – based on the sample of people I contacted in connection with this essay who were not keen to do an interview – is that there were not so many. Ambrose Mendy identified one person who, in his view, could have been a powerful force for acceptance – and perhaps changed the course of Justin's career altogether. The history of football could have been very different, said Mendy, 'if Brian Clough had acknowledged and embraced Justin as a human being'. When he signed Justin from Norwich City, Clough had already won the European Cup in consecutive seasons with Nottingham Forest, and was one of the game's most influential voices. He was a cultural icon, beloved on the talk-show circuit and far beyond Britain, so well known for his wit that Muhammad Ali joyfully sparred with him on late-night television. If anyone could have spoken for Justin, said Ambrose, it was Clough. But, as Clough himself later admitted in his autobiography, 'I had a responsibility towards [Justin] because he was under my jurisdiction as the manager of the club, and I gave him nothing.'

When I spoke to Mendy, his fury with Clough was as intense as a forest fire. He made clear that there was no homophobia towards Justin in the Forest dressing room – due in part to Justin's imposing physique – and that any outspoken bigotry came repeatedly from Clough himself, who referred to him as 'a bloody poof' in front of his fellow players. A year after being signed by Clough, Justin was sold to neighbouring Notts County

Justin Fashanu's prolific form and rare talent resulted in his transfer to Nottingham Forest. He commanded a £1 million pound transfer fee – a sum that made him Britain's most expensive Black footballer.

for a tenth of his purchase price, and his confidence was decimated too. Footage from that period shows him slashing wildly at the ball with his favoured right foot, sending the ball soaring safely high or wide of goal. It makes for a tragic contrast with his body language when, ten days before his nineteenth birthday, he scored the goal that made him famous. On that day in February 1980, playing for Norwich City against league champions Liverpool, he had conjured a turn and volley of rare magnificence; his limbs moving as easily and as elegantly as a silk flag in the breeze. 'Football never saw sixty-five per cent of the potential of Justin,' said Mendy. 'And all of the time he was within his shell, he did crazy things.' Mendy recalled the time when Justin made a great show of dating Julie Goodyear, the actress who played Bet Lynch in *Coronation Street*. 'That was a charade, a masquerade,' he said – the mask firmly in place.

On one occasion, Mendy's support of Justin even took physical form, as he found himself in an altercation with a manager. Justin had returned from surgery in the USA, after which he was at only eighty per cent of his physical peak but more than smart enough to make up for any inhibited movements. He went up for trials at Manchester City, where 'he played in three reserve games and scored a hat-trick, a hat-trick and two goals'. While City were deliberating over whether to make an offer, Ambrose received a call from another manager. That manager, having heard of Justin's goalscoring exploits, said that his club were very keen to sign him, and that he would speak to his chairman. A few days later, Mendy went to the club in question to make the final arrangements for Justin's contract only to find the manager in a very different mood:

> All of a sudden I hear a kerfuffle near the boardroom, and [the manager] is coming in my direction, and his eyes are

> bulging. 'What have you fucking done to me, what have you done? You fucking knew this!' And I said, 'Slow down, what the hell are you talking about?' [And he replied] 'He's a fucking poof! He's a poof! You know, he's a shit-shoveller!' This is what he said. So I knocked him out.

If it had been left to Justin, he would not have thrown any punches. As his brother John notes, Justin was 'a peacemaker'. By John's own admission, when it came to the use of violence in football, he was much more proactive than his older brother. For John, life was about striking a blow at the world before the world could strike a blow at you. He was so renowned for his combative approach to the game that he was nicknamed 'Fash the Bash', a reputation he was proud to indulge and promote. He was one of the figureheads of Wimbledon FC, football's proudest outlaws, whose legend was established when they defeated the heavily favoured Liverpool 1–0 in the 1988 FA Cup Final. The team were in turn known as 'The Crazy Gang', and keenly marketed themselves as an aggressive, hard-running outfit who could out-brawl many of their opponents. Yet there always seemed to be much more to John than mere brawn. In several of his highlights from that period, he can be seen floating delicate chips over the heads of opposition goalkeepers, or sending them the wrong way from the penalty spot after a single-step run-up.

For all of his talk of being the tough guy, I wondered if the use of force had always come naturally to him. I wondered if his hyper-aggressive persona – a finely controlled one, which has seen him acquire black belt-level expertise in four martial arts – was truly him, or a response to oppressive circumstances. I asked him as much, and he explained how life had been for him and Justin as children in Norfolk: 'Bear in mind, we were living in a rural area, and Blacks were unheard of ... I couldn't understand why, when I was going to school, I was consistently bullied and beaten up for many, many years. And I think that's what gave me that hardness, that strength, [to make me] into who I am today.'

John and Justin's football careers contain enough parallels that, by looking at John's path through the game, we can gain some idea of the racial obstacles Justin must have faced. Most strikingly, John told me the story of when he joined a club in the 1980s:

> I was taken into the dressing room to shake everybody's hand, and as I stretched my hand out to meet everybody, nobody wanted to shake my hand ... There was a lot of racism towards me. My own teammates were calling me 'nigger'. It was my nickname. Nigger. Nigger. So, the away players would call me 'nigger', and the home players would call me 'nigger'. And this was a pattern at many of the football clubs I played for. And the way that I established myself was to pick the hardest man at the club, and get into a good fight with him, and beat the hell out of him. And then people would go, 'Whoa, now you've got our respect, Fash.' And it's always been that sort of way, for me to become the captain. And most of the teams I've been to, I've been the captain.

Both John and Justin were keen to court publicity (both of them were very comfortable in front of cameras and television audiences). John got precisely the coverage he wanted: he was portrayed as a fearsome athlete with a witty side, a persona he would eventually weave into a hugely successful career as a presenter on ITV's *Gladiators*, a sports entertainment game show that he co-hosted for much of the nineties. Justin, by contrast, was utterly unable to control the narratives about him, and found himself immersed in scandal. In 1990, he agreed to a lucrative and exclusive interview with *The Sun*, in which he revealed that he had had an affair with a married Conservative Party politician. The resulting media inferno tore through the bond between the two brothers, with John at first regarding it as nothing more than a publicity stunt to steal his growing limelight. In a 2019 interview with the *Mail on Sunday*,[2] John recalled his reaction to the news: 'Stop showing off. You're trying to take my glory. You're not going to do it. I'm the No1 footballer, I've taken your position, I'm now in the Premiership and playing for England. You're now smoking out, having injuries and you just want to take my platform.'

It was only in time that John would understand that Justin's desire to come out was rooted in a need to be free from the burden of silence. While John refers in that same interview to 'sibling rivalry', it is not clear from speaking to Ambrose Mendy, who knew the brothers better than most people did, that there was much rivalry from Justin's side. The picture is instead one of John adoring his older brother while also being envious, to an extent, of the ease with which Justin at first moved through the game. Ambrose spoke of the difference in their levels of natural ability, remarking that, whereas John had to work tirelessly on his craft, 'Justin was blessed.'

John's response to his brother's sexuality comes in for harsh criticism today – not least from John himself. (Ironically, the one club of the era that could probably have protected Justin was the one that John played for – the Crazy Gang, who were brash, resolutely themselves, and had no respect for received wisdom.) While John believes that he should have helped Justin more, Mendy's judgement is more measured. 'They did as much as they could have done for each other,' he told me, pointing to the fact that John frequently gave Justin money when his career faltered time and again. Yet there was probably still an emotional component of support that was lacking from John. This was, after all, a period when homophobia in Justin's own community was at radioactive levels. In response to Justin's coming out, Tony Sewell, a columnist for *The Voice* – the UK's only national weekly Afro-Caribbean newspaper – wrote that 'We heteros are sick and tired of tortured queens playing hide and seek around their closets. Homosexuals are the greatest queer-bashers around. No other group of people are so preoccupied with making their own sexuality look dirty.' It would take Sewell thirty years to publicly retract these remarks, and only after they were presented to him by *The Guardian*.[3] Sewell's apology came upon his appointment as chair of the government's commission on race and ethnic disparities in 2020, proving that – at least in some areas of modern Britain – failing to atone for extreme homophobia is still no barrier to career progress.

As John reflected on these events, it became clear that his relationship with his brother was warm and affectionate, but also – on some level – perhaps still tinged with regret, and a little unresolved. At one point, when assessing their careers, he felt the need to assert that his record proved that he had been 'the better player'. At another, there was a sense that he thought that Justin could have done more to help himself, perhaps through greater use of secrecy. John recalled asking Justin, '"Why do you feel the urge to have to broadcast [your sexuality], to bring the spotlight on yourself, when you're a wonderful player and a lovely person?" Because then all people say is "He's gay, he's a gay Black footballer." Not good.' Finally, though, he seemed to understand that the scale of the challenge faced by Justin was possibly beyond him:

> You've got two very big hills to climb – well, not even hills for goodness' sake, I would say mountains. You're black. And

you're gay. Oh, my goodness me. And I made some mistakes when I was with Justin, trying to look after Justin, trying to help him, because I'm sorry to say that even I couldn't accept him. And if your own brother can't accept that his brother's gay, then what do you think other people are going to think as well?

Though John and Justin's lives had very different trajectories – by the time Justin died, in 1998, the brothers had at one point gone over seven years without speaking – there is one area in which they remained closely aligned: the business of finding the net. John scored 149 times in 396 games at professional level (including two appearances for England's senior team), an average of 0.38 goals per game. Justin scored 138 times in

Justin Fashanu slices his birthday cake along with his brother, John, and a large group of their friends.

376 professional games (eleven of which were for England's under-21 side), an average of 0.37 goals per game. The two of them even played for the same club in New Zealand, albeit fifteen years apart: Miramar Rangers, where they were both coached by the legendary David Farrington. Even there they were similarly prolific, with John scoring fifteen goals in eleven games in the 1982 season, and Justin scoring twelve goals in eighteen appearances in 1997. Perhaps there is another far gentler and more innocent universe where John and Justin, free from the ravages of bigotry and able to play to their full potential, end up appearing several times for England, maybe even playing together at Wembley.

If that universe exists, it is infinitely distant from our one in which, Mendy noted, Justin's aforementioned knee injury – so serious that he never fully recovered from it – was aggravated because several physicians in the early nineties were unwilling even to touch him. Justin's emergence as a potentially elite footballer coincided almost exactly with the emergence of the AIDS epidemic, which at the time was associated almost exclusively with gay men. In 1988, the UK was so prejudiced against gay people that its Conservative government, under the infamous Section 28 of that year's Local Government Act, decreed that homosexuality should not be promoted in schools. Around the same time that Justin came out as gay, it was still considered taboo to hug someone who was HIV-positive. This unfortunate confluence of events meant that Justin, in the words of Mendy, was frequently treated 'as if he had Ebola'.

Given Justin's later embrace of Christianity, it is grimly fitting that the story of his life and early death seems to mirror the lyrics of one of the most famous African-American spirituals, 'Sinner Man', the best-known version of which was sung by Nina Simone. The unnamed protagonist runs from place to place – from the rock, to the river, to the sea – looking for shelter and comfort, but is unable to find respite anywhere they turn. Eventually they run to the Lord, who turns them away and tells them to run to the Devil. When they get to the Devil, he is waiting for them. It could be that Justin felt like the Sinner Man of his era, rushing everywhere in search of help but finding that almost no one would offer assistance. It was yet another cruel twist to his tale: society was in the wrong, but he was forced to beg society for absolution. According to Other Stories, an LGBT history project run by the charity Derbyshire LGBT+, Justin observed that 'Friends who I'd ... known for many, many years, who'd become managers, and coaches, and chairmen, and directors – suddenly the doors shut. So, there was a lot of backlash. I couldn't get a job. The bottom line was I couldn't get a job.' Few wanted to be tainted by association with him. And so Justin carried on fleeing, from the rock to the river to the sea, only to end up not seeking out the Devil but instead doing something worse: taking a long, overwhelming look at his life up until that point.

In view of everything that Justin had been through, his alleged actions in the final chapter of his life are all the more inexcusable. In April 1998, he was charged with sexually assaulting a seventeen-year-old boy in the US state of Maryland, a claim that, according to the court documents, was supported by medical evidence. Justin fled the country after being questioned by police, knowing that a conviction could lead to imprisonment for up to twenty years and confiding in those who knew him that, as a gay man, he did not think he would get a fair trial. He was found dead a month later in a garage in East London, having hanged himself. In a life spent fleeing for safer havens, Justin's final act on earth was to flee himself. When his accuser was given the news of his death, he told *The Baltimore Sun* that he had 'a lot of mixed feelings ... I feel bad he did it to himself. But I'm also disgusted about what he did to me. I'm upset that I didn't get to see him go through trial, see justice. I didn't get to confront him, ask him why he did it.'

Sometimes when I think of Justin Fashanu, I think of 'Oumuamua. Other times, though, I think *he wasn't some mystical, celestial object: he was utterly human.* I think of people like his accuser, whose obvious suffering would have been exacerbated by Justin's fame. I think that, unlike 'Oumuamua, Justin did not manage to fly free after all. Though his odyssey took him across the world, he came full circle, dying in Shoreditch, only a few miles from his birthplace of Hackney.

Since Justin's death, there have been other openly gay players in the men's game: Swedish footballer Anton Hysén in 2011, American Robbie Rogers and German Thomas Hitzlsperger in 2013. Perhaps tellingly, Rogers and Hitzlsperger came out either close to or after their retirement, while Hysén, who came out at twenty-one, has generally played for clubs that are unhindered by the glare of huge publicity. This suggests that more footballers would have taken Mendy's two-pronged advice: build strong support networks within the game and 'Come out when you're good and ready to come out.' The fact that Hitzlsperger would go on to become the director of football at VfB Stuttgart, one of Germany's most successful clubs, shows that significant progress has been made behind the scenes, even if gay players are still wary of being subjected to the full glare of social media and the wider public. There has still not been another openly gay Black footballer since Justin stepped forward, indicating that the double burden of racism and homophobia is still too great to bear.

The one thing that resonates most strongly throughout Justin's story is the silence – the silence of those who could have aided him more at certain points in his life but didn't. Mendy was still keen to interrogate the leading players of Justin's generation, who stood by and watched his ostracism even though their influence could have changed so much. 'What does it feel like to know that you were in close proximity with the first openly gay Black footballer?' said Mendy. He continued:

> What did you do? That's what I want to ask everybody. All Justin needed, as well as an arm round his shoulder, was an acceptance. He was rejected every moment of his life. There was not one day of his life this boy was not rejected. You've only got to look at every club that he went to: he left, because he wasn't wanted.

I wondered when Mendy had last seen Justin.

'Probably the year before he died.'

Was he in a better place when you saw him?

'Justin was doing what Justin was always doing. He was on his way somewhere. He was in between two points.'

'You know', Mendy went on, 'the greatest labour-saving device ever invented is the word "tomorrow". Domani, mañana, demain ... Tomorrow. Tomorrow. And there's that famous title, "tomorrow never comes". In many respects, that's the irony of Justin's life: tomorrow never came.'

IAN WRIGHT

Life at the Vanguard, Again and Again

Thomas Theodore

The morning I'm due to speak with Ian Wright, paramedics rush my grandad to Barnet Hospital. He'd been experiencing breathing difficulties and tested positive for COVID-19.

My grandad's eighty-two and – despite maintaining a teenage demeanour – is kept alive by a pacemaker (Saint Lucia's first – he had it fitted amid a health scare on holiday a decade ago) and a luridly colourful cocktail of medication (for diabetes, among other things). Stooping at about five foot ten, he's every inch the patient public healthcare experts would describe as having – to use modern parlance – serious underlying health conditions.

I'm WhatsApping my aunt for updates, while awaiting the final interview confirmation from Wright's manager. Just after midday, Wright's face appears on Zoom. For just under ninety minutes, 13,500 rapidly spoken words of transcript, Ian Wright is honest, straight-talking and life-affirming.

During a professional football career that ended almost twenty-one years ago, Ian Wright scored 333 goals.

Goals at the end of dribbles, long-range drives, one-on-ones, a few headers, some penalties, elegant chips and scrappy tap-ins: Ian Wright wasn't fussy. Fizzing with vivacity, he celebrated almost every single one, arms thrown aloft, grinning, dancing, almost as if through semaphore and gesticulation he was asking the crowd: 'did you just see THAT?'

Wright turned professional late – aged twenty-one he was still playing in South East London's Sunday leagues – but through hard work, willpower and charisma he became British football's first Black superstar: the lightning bolt in boring, boring Arsenal, the attention-seeking energy flash at the dawn of the Premier League.

There were successful Black footballers before Ian Wright, but none were like him: the way he spoke in interviews, the way he carried himself on the pitch, as well as the scoring and the celebrating; unadulterated black expression.

Wright's goals won games, they won him domestic trophies, a European trophy and thirty-three England caps, but that was all over two decades ago, and the sport's moved on. As remarkable as his playing achievements has been his ability to transition beyond retirement and remain relevant in this new footballing age.

This older, wiser Wright has grown into a role as a popular elder in Black British public life. To work out how Wright has 'retired' so successfully, let's start in the middle.

//

Under the floodlights at Filbert Street, Arsenal's number 8 Paul Davis intercepts a pass from Leicester City's Colin Gibson and slides a gentle diagonal ball from the edge of the centre circle towards the left corner of the penalty box.

Ian Wright, wearing number 9 and playing his first game for Arsenal that night, loops his run around the pass, and, as the ball decelerates, attempts to cut it back onto his right foot. He slips over on the turf, but – while propped up by his right arm – manages to use his left foot to nudge the ball to the spot he originally intended. The instant he regains his footing, he hits a low shot towards the goal's opposite corner.

Wright strikes the ball when positioned precisely between television camera and far post, meaning that – whether you're watching this Rumbelows Cup second-round, first-leg tie live from an armchair in September 1991, or 'Ian Wright scores on his debut vs Leicester City' on YouTube nearly thirty years later – you have the luxury of seeing exactly where the ball's heading. The shot bounces off the inside of the post and into the net. Arsenal take a 1–0 lead.

The darting run, the retreating centre backs, the improvisation, the speed of thought, the ball in the bottom corner, then that grin. Wright throws both arms aloft in celebration and his new teammate Paul Merson embraces him briefly, before running back for the kick-off.

Wright lingers at the edge of the box and is soon surrounded by four more of his new teammates. 'I scored the goal, David Rocastle came over, then Michael Thomas, Kevin Campbell, and Paul Davis, all Black South Londoners,' Wright recalled. 'There's a picture of us at Leicester in the bruised banana,' as Arsenal's fondly remembered black-and-yellow-chevroned away shirt became known.

Wright settled quickly at Arsenal, winning the league's Golden Boot in his first season north of the river and quickly justifying the substantial £2.5 million transfer fee the club had paid Crystal Palace for his services. He credits the team's nucleus of Black South Londoners, all of whom had won the league title the previous season, as vital to his instant success in North London:

> We used to go to the raves and the clubs around South London, drinking our rum and black or Bacardi and Coke and doing our stuff. It was very comfortable. We had so much that we could relate to with each other – it was almost like being in one of our mum's kitchens, or the kitchen of a blues dance, just in there talking about stuff.

Wright celebrates scoring on his Arsenal debut against Leicester with his close friend, the late David Rocastle, and Michael Thomas, Kevin Campbell and Paul Davis. The five men formed a nucleus of Black South Londoners in the Arsenal dressing room.

> When we were younger we were in the minority, you didn't always have many Black players. When I was at Palace, I was sometimes the only Black guy in the team. At Arsenal we were always together, all five of us were always in the team.
>
> It was brilliant, we could talk how we wanted to talk, we could say what we wanted to say, hold our own against anybody in there, so we could join in, all have the banter and that. I only spent a year with David, then Michael Thomas went on to Liverpool, Paul Davis was eased out. Me and Kevin were together for a little while, but then Kevin left. I didn't realise it, but seriously, it was a beautiful time.

I'm too young to recall Arsenal's core of Black South Londoners, but anyone who's been in an unfamiliar and daunting situation can relate to the reassurance Wright felt.

This group of players emerged and played amid a climate of abuse from away terraces, and the natural camaraderie and friendship they formed created a professional footballing environment in which Wright could be successful *and* be himself – a promise that it was possible to do it all without compromise.

//

My grandad came to Britain from Saint Lucia aboard the SS *Columbie*. It was 1954, he was sixteen years old and spent the first 18 months of his new life in London washing dishes at the Trocadero. He bought a bicycle and began learning his way around London, not like a kid on a Boris Bike nor a new arrival eager to see the sights of 'The Mother Country', my grandad cycled aggressively. He was preparing to take The Knowledge – the series of tests a prospective black taxi driver must pass in order to receive their licence. Immediately able to reject the notion that the streets were paved with anything but tarmac and asphalt, if London was to be the place for him, its roads he'd have to learn to navigate. Make no bones, he'd come here to work.

I'm interested in Wright's retirement because my grandad – who, at the time of writing, is out of hospital and slowly and steadily recovering at home – has never retired, nor has my grandmother. Up to six nights a week, for sixty-five years, my grandad has put on a suit and driven his taxi around London. I understand that retirement might be daunting or unprecedented, but not gonna lie, I'm lowkey hoping Wrighty's got some tips.

//

You probably know Ian Wright's story, the schoolboy embraced by his teacher Mr Pigden, rejected by Brighton, but eventually deemed good enough for Steve Coppell's Crystal Palace. Aged twenty-two, Wright quit his job in a factory and started making up for lost time, scoring over 100 goals for Palace and making two trips to Wembley before George Graham signed him for Arsenal.

That goal away to Leicester City was the first of 185 for the team, and in his first three years at Highbury, Wright won an FA Cup, a League Cup and a UEFA Cup Winners' Cup. In 1996, Arsène Wenger became Arsenal manager and Wright, then in his thirties but still that berserk bundle of energy, completed his journey from South London to the stratosphere with Dennis Bergkamp and Marc Overmars, Patrick Vieira and Emmanuel Petit.

If you don't remember the times, then watch the clips. Ian Wright Wright Wright 179, just done it swoosh, celebrating a goal too early, a Premier League and FA Cup double, playing off the last man, winding up the away fans, a chip on his shoulder, a gold-toothed grin, I love the lads, IAN WRIGHT WRIGHT WRIGHT the words to the chant, a pyramid on the Highbury scoreboards.

//

In 2000, Ian Wright appeared on *This Is Your Life*.* Guests who surprised him included Wenger, boxer Lennox Lewis,

* For the benefit of younger readers, *This Is Your Life* was a long-running show from a more innocent TV age on which a famous person and a presenter, at the time an old dude named Michael Aspel, would stand in front of a studio audience. Aspel held a red book and narrated the famous person's story while the famous person was surprised on stage by important people from their life. Pretty cute, huh? Yeah, we've come a long way since the millennium. Older readers, alongside those mentioned, Ian Wright was also surprised by Dale Winton, Esther Rantzen and Jeremy Beadle.

Ian Wright celebrates breaking Arsenal's goalscoring record in 1997. He remains the club's second-highest scorer of all time.

singer and fellow South Londoner Maxi Priest, plus former teammates Tony Adams and Mark Bright. Also featured in the episode – a sweeping, tearful eulogy to his career – were Wright's young family, with the eldest two boys, Shaun and Bradley, both about to embark upon their own professional footballing journeys.

The role Wright played in his sons' early careers is central to understanding his relationship with today's young Premier

League stars. Long before he became Uncle Ian – guide and counsel to the Premier League's modern players – he was a father to Black footballers.

Initially, Wright would watch Shaun and Bradley's matches from afar, keen to protect them from the unwanted attention of opposition players or parents. But, as both boys began to demonstrate talent, Wright realised that the first half of their hyphenated surname was going to loom over them, so decided he'd turn his celebrity to his boys' advantage.

Sitting with them in the car on the way home, if they'd found a game tough and complained that they were under heightened scrutiny because of their Arsenal-star dad, he'd remind them:

> Look, people pay to watch footballers. If you want to be a footballer, you have to get used to people watching you. It's got nothing to do with me, I'm just your dad watching. But don't worry about who's watching. Worry about what you're contributing. What did you do good in the game? Did you play any one-twos? Did you encourage anyone?

Winger Shaun's ability to ride tackles while dribbling, and forward Bradley's ability to score and bring teammates into play, started to attract the interest of professional clubs. But, like Ian, they were undersized for their positions, and as teenagers both were rejected by Nottingham Forest:

> I just thought to myself, *You don't know what to say, so don't lie to them.* Just say 'That's what happens, it's people's opinion, they're entitled to their opinion and people make mistakes. I proved people wrong. I proved they made a mistake with me. That's what you've got to go and do, because if you love playing and that's what you want to do,

then you have to take the bad times with the good. *This* is a bad time.' They worked twice as hard, and bam, it happened for them.

Football forces young people to navigate unprecedented situations. It's a world filled with advisers eager to bend the ears of young players. There's no roadmap. But Wright's honest, straight-talking approach to football parenting worked out well. Shaun Wright-Phillips won two FA Cups and a Premier League title, and retired with 36 England caps, three more than his father, while younger brother Bradley Wright-Phillips – who plays for Columbus Crew in the USA – is currently the sixth-highest scorer in Major League Soccer history.

//

Retirement abruptly challenges footballers to move beyond the sport that has provided them with decades of structure and public validation. Whether it happens because they fail to recover from an injury, they're released from a contract and no other clubs are interested in signing them, or they get to bow out on their own terms after a testimonial match, by their mid-thirties, all players have to confront a life beyond the game.

Even before he'd finished playing, Wright went into television – what he called the 'shiny floor world'. He presented a chat show called *Friday Night's All Wright* from 1998 to 2000, as he saw out the final years of his playing career:

> It was still an arena where there was a spotlight on you. I wasn't afraid of the idea of doing a light entertainment television show. I interviewed Denzel Washington, Will Smith. Beyoncé came on the show with Destiny's Child. So,

> I was in a place where my confidence was really high, really high. The television gave me that adulation I was craving.
>
> At three o'clock on a Saturday afternoon, something happens for years afterwards, autopilot in your body. I missed football so much, even when I was doing all these interviews with all the famous people, I was still empty. It was a weird time. I was still getting recognition, but it wasn't how I thought it was going to be. But at the time, as a Black footballer, coming from where I come from, straight into a ten o'clock show? There was a DJ, there was a live audience, it was very street.

Wright – inexperienced and openly winging it – attracted animosity. Veteran talk-show host Michael Parkinson, who had only recently returned to screens, was quick to lash out, calling Wright 'a pillock' and accusing him of having a 'careless attitude' both in *The Times* and in a tirade on BBC Radio 5 Live.[1] 'I was literally just doing it off personality,' said Wright. 'I didn't have anyone to speak to. Who was I going to ask about this and that?'

Trinidad-born newsreader Trevor McDonald, who'd been a guest on the second season of *Friday Night's All Wright*, reached out: 'When Parkinson came hard, [McDonald] said "Fuck 'em, don't give a fuck what they say." And to hear Trevor McDonald swear, it's beautiful.' Wright can still recite the words of advice he was offered:

> He said, 'You carry on doing what you're doing, and do not give them the opportunity or the excuses where you have not done the work, so they can point a finger at you. Do the work, do all that stuff, whatever you have to read, whatever you have to find out, to make sure that when you're on there, you're factual. And then you put your personality

> across, which none of them have got, then they cannot touch you. They'll come for you like he's come for you. He's afraid of you, he's afraid that you are now embarrassing him. Everything [Parkinson's] done was magnificent for all these years. But you've come a different way, so you've got to understand that you're going to get that kind of negativity. Don't give them the excuse to bring you down.'

Friday Night's All Wright was a celebration of a burgeoning Black British culture, an indirect forbear to Channel 4's *The Big Narstie Show*. While Wright's inexperience ultimately led to his show's cancellation, a dialled-up anarchic amateurism is a key tenet of Narstie's contemporary appeal.

Wright's 2019 appearance on *The Big Narstie Show* demonstrated the extent to which times have changed. Sitting on

When Michael Parkinson criticised Ian Wright and his television chat show, *Friday Night's All Wright*, Trevor McDonald rang to offer him support.

the couch beside fellow guest Stephen Fry, Wright is questioned about his experience presenting a show two decades earlier. Mid-answer, Narstie interrupts to announce his in-ear monitor is malfunctioning, a debacle ensues and Wright joins in the chaos, causing laughter among the studio audience – it's exactly the kind of hijinks they're there to witness.

We're now in a TV era where establishment and anti-establishment can comfortably sit side by side, an era Ian Wright has played a role in bringing about. In the nineties, there was little precedent. There was *The Arsenio Hall Show* (1989–94) in the USA. In the UK, shows like *Desmond's* (1989–94) or *The Real McCoy* (1991–96) were recorded in front of studio audiences and introduced viewers to depictions of Black British life, but their diverse casts were trained actors and comedians. Wright was still a footballer, driving from training to the TV studio and playing matches on Saturdays.

The second season of *Friday Night's All Wright* coincided with the only season of *The Richard Blackwood Show* (1999–2001), Channel 4's soon-aborted attempt to find a Black talk show host. Rapport with the guests may have come naturally, but for Wright and Blackwood there were few role models, little structure and, beyond McDonald, few people prepared to offer honest advice.

After brief stints playing for West Ham, Nottingham Forest, Celtic and finally Burnley, Wright retired in 2000. When it came to his life after the game, there was no definite path. He wasn't as rich as today's retirees, but he was still a recognised public figure. Looking back, he feels like his agents took a short-term approach, pressuring him into more TV jobs that he was unprepared for:

> They were about the money they could make. I could have done my coaching badges, but they did everything they could

to steer me away from that because it would have stopped all the commission they were earning from the television shows. I was on TV too much at a time. If you're on TV that much, and you haven't done enough research, you're gonna start talking a lot of shit, you're going to start talking for the sake of talking. They were just on the take, they didn't care how long I'd last. I felt that for many years, being used by agents. It felt like going back to when I was younger: people didn't really want you for you, but for what you could give, or offer, and that's never a nice feeling. Those were the things I thought about a lot when I retired and it was always a very lonely feeling.

//

In September 1997, Wright had become the Arsenal's all-time top goalscorer, surpassing the tally of 178 set by Cliff Bastin in 1939. In May 1998, Arsenal won both the Premier League and the FA Cup, Wright left the club in the summer following the 1997–98 season.

Manager Arsène Wenger swept changes through English football. His first double-winning side combined experienced senior players, revitalised by changes to training and diet, with new, dynamic talent from overseas. Following Wright's departure, Arsenal repeated the league and cup double in 2001–02, and in 2003–04 they won the Premier League without losing a game – the first club to achieve 'invincibility' in over 100 years. In October 2005, Ian Wright's goalscoring record was broken by French forward Thierry Henry, who'd arrived at the club from Juventus six years earlier. Later in the 2005–06 season, Arsenal reached the Champions League Final and left Highbury, their home for ninety-three years, for the Emirates Stadium.

'It was very easy for the fans, especially from 2002 to that Champions League Final,' Wright told me. 'It was hard to be an ex-player. Even our era under Wenger was cast aside because of the magnificence of The Invincibles.' He's right. I'm an Arsenal fan, and in those moments there was no need to dwell on the past. Wenger's breathtaking, freeform playing style made George Graham's ground-out defensive displays, an Ian Wright goal the only highlight in a 1–0 win, feel like ancient history.

//

I remember seeing Wright return for Tony Adams's (second) testimonial against Celtic in 2002. A rainy May night, at the end of Wenger's second double-winning season, Highbury sung in chorus, jubilant after clinching the Premier League title in Manchester and winning the FA Cup in Cardiff just days earlier. In the second half, Wright came off the bench. He'd warmed up to a huge ovation and looked eager as ever to get involved. Late in the game, Arsenal midfielder Patrick Vieira floated a gentle diagonal ball from the edge of the centre circle towards the left corner of the penalty box.

The stadium collectively drew breath as Wright attempted to latch onto the pass but – almost forty and two years retired – his legs began to give way. He stumbled and fell to the turf, but unlike that night at Leicester City over a decade before, couldn't regain balance in time, the game moved on. Wright saw the funny side, turned and grinned at the North Bank. 'IAN WRIGHT WRIGHT WRIGHT' rang out around the stands.

My dad drove us home around the North Circular, the windscreen wipers rocking back and forth, heating on full blast, me steaming up the windows talking enthusiastically about the game. At that moment, Wright's cameo barely registered, I was fourteen and I thought Arsenal were going to stay that good forever. 'It was a strange time,' Wright recalls:

> It wasn't that [the fans] didn't care about what *we'd* done. [The team] were just playing such amazing stuff that the fans were miles too busy with what the team were doing. It was very easy to get really hedonistic on that vibe, because it was football from a different planet. My relationship with the club at the time was very much like, 'Hey, err ... umm ... how's it going?!' They weren't interested in anything else, because it was too brilliant, it was too orgasmic, it was fantastic.

When talking about the era, Wright began to sound less like a former player, and more like a fan:

> It took us to such a high that I'm not sure we'll ever reach again, if we're going to be totally honest. It's going to take us many, many years to reach the kind of stratospheric football we were playing at that time.

Since moving to the Emirates, Arsenal have struggled to match the heights of that period. To create atmosphere and appease a demanding fanbase whose standards were warped by the late-Highbury era, the club increasingly appeals to its history. In 2011, Arsenal began unveiling statues honouring influential figures in the club's story. Thierry Henry is cast in bronze, knee sliding after gliding through Tottenham's entire midfield and defence. Dennis Bergkamp is suspended in mid-air, extending his right foot to pluck the ball out of the sky against Newcastle United. Tony Adams stands with arms aloft, walking off into the sunset after scoring against Everton in 1998. Ken Friar, a longstanding member of the club's board – who rose from selling match day tickets in the 1950s to his current position as lifetime president – is depicted as a schoolboy. A figure of Herbert Chapman stands outside the grounds, while inside the stadium there's a bust of Wenger – tributes to the two great managerial modernisers in the club's history.

So far there's no statue of Wright, who was voted fourth behind Henry, Bergkamp and Adams in a 2008 club-run poll of the Arsenal's greatest ever players. But he's found more useful, informal, improvised ways to weave himself into the fabric of modern, Emirates-era Arsenal.

Over the past three seasons – and for the first time since the advent of the Premier League – a group of players have emerged from Arsenal's youth academy and become members of the first-team squad: Joe Willock, Reiss Nelson, Ainsley Maitland-Niles, Eddie Nketiah, and Bukayo Saka. In 2020–21, Saka aside, this quintet of Black Londoners have been largely utilised in the Europa League or off the substitutes' bench. If they're hungry to achieve a similar level of success to the group of Black players who embraced Wright upon his Arsenal debut thirty years ago, then Wright's there to help.

Players contact him on Instagram or WhatsApp, and he often follows up their messages with a phone call. This availability has earned him the loving nickname 'Uncle Ian' among both Arsenal and England's young players:

> I think they see a Black player they recognise and relate to. I tell them exactly what I need to tell them about their game, about what's going to happen when they start getting a bit more success. Anything that they're going to go through, I've been through, and I let them know it with honesty. Do you need to buy that car? Do you need to be posting that on social media? What are you focusing on at the training

ground? How hard are you working on that? If you're not in the team, how hard are you training for the manager to see that you deserve a chance?

I'll tell Reiss, 'You're desperate to get in the team, we've got an underperforming player at the minute in [Nicolas] Pépé. Yes, he cost £72 million but you've still got an opportunity to perform and get in there, and a manager that will give you an opportunity.' I say, 'If you are on corners, free kicks when you come on, then you make sure you put them in the areas that the manager wants you to put them in. If the boss wants you on free kicks and corners and all the set pieces, then if you're not doing at least thirty or forty of them after every training session to make sure you hit the mark, then you will be eased out, because you're not trying to progress yourself and you're not trying to get better.'

The manager will tell them things and, yes, they will listen to him. But when they hear it from outside and you give it to them in a real way, it makes them realise, *You are at Arsenal now, but if you do not take this opportunity, it'll not be long before you're at Bournemouth*. It all happens very quickly, just like that. Look at Maitland-Niles: I'm pleased he's stopped saying things like, 'I don't want to play right-back.' Look, you're playing, that's what's got you into the England set-up. People might say, 'But yeah, what position are you?' It doesn't make any difference, he's got into the England side on what he's capable of doing for the team.

//

The positionally ambiguous Ainsley Maitland-Niles was called up to the August 2020 England squad alongside his teenage Arsenal teammate Bukayo Saka. They are among fifteen black and mixed-race players included in England manager Gareth Southgate's recent squads. Young and talented Premier League footballers often mention representing their country among their footballing ambitions, but an international call-up is rarely without precedent.

Both Maitland-Niles and Saka represented England at five junior levels before breaking into the full squad, and both spent their teens attending age-group camps at St George's Park, England's national football centre. For today's Black players, even in the season of taking a knee, pulling on an England shirt and running out at Wembley is less a political act and more a rite of passage.

Wright can talk excitedly about young English players, which you'd expect from a pundit, but he played for England in a different era. For previous generations, navigating national identity has required more improvisation.

//

My grandad, like those who travelled to the UK following the Nationality Act 1948, arrived a British citizen. Despite the setbacks he's faced – the few incidents I've gleaned from his stories, the entire iceberg of racism he never told me about, the mistreatment at the hands of several Home Offices – he's proudly British. He loves PG Tips, the Queen, Bruce Forsyth and Derek 'Del Boy' Trotter, and remains determined to uphold his side of the bargain that brought him on a two-week, one-way trip across the North Atlantic seven decades ago.

He also listens to rocksteady and still talks about *Roots* and Alex Pascall's show on BBC Radio London. He once made me co-write a letter to former Ghanaian President Jerry John Rawlings, and hung on the wall is photographic evidence of his brief friendship with Sobhuza II, who was the king of Swaziland for eighty-two years. Go to my grandparents' house and you'll get cassava bread and baked beans for breakfast, or Sunday lunch served with carrots, peas, plantain and dasheen. Walk quietly enough along a corridor and you'll hear them speaking patois; the moment you get into earshot they'll switch, mid-sentence, to English.

This kind of Englishness might be familiar to readers from Black Caribbean backgrounds. I find it comforting, but it's also sometimes confusing in its contradictory nature. It's a loose, improvised forbear to my modern identity politics, based on experiences that overlap, intertwine and eventually creolise.

Academic Paul Gilroy has written frequently and eloquently on the complicated relationship between Blackness and English national identity. In his 1990 essay 'Art of Darkness' (a longer version of which appears in his 1993 book *Small Acts: Thoughts on the Politics of Black Cultures*), he mentions Wright's revelation that he'd cried with pride while putting on his England shirt before a B-team fixture in 1989.

Gilroy positions Wright alongside musician Jazzie B and artist Sonia Boyce as key Black figures at the forefront of a search for a more pluralistic sense of Englishness. Gilroy describes the trio's work as 'part of a wider struggle to affiliate with England, and in doing so, [they] change what it means to be English. The young, gifted and black Britons are not naive. The impact of a diaspora sensibility on their lives means that they can readily comprehend the limitations of national identities as such.' Against this backdrop, and seeking a shift away from racial absolutism and narrow definitions of Englishness, Gilroy framed their work as 'part of the long, micro-political task of re-coding the cultural core of national life', by which 'the fissures, stress cracks and structural fatigue in the edifices of Englishness become more interesting and acquire their own beauty'.[2]

Wright lists playing for England among his proudest achievements, actively revelling in the bothness of his Black-English identity. We all have to navigate a changing relationship with the country of our birth, or the country we live in. Most of us can go about this navigation in private and fairly unchallenged, but in 1991 pulling on an England shirt, belting out 'God Save the Queen' and playing for your country must have forced that relationship into an unusual position.

> It just upset the right kind of person, when I let them know how much I loved England. Yes, my heritage is Jamaica, but I'm England. People for some reason can't put it together that you're Black and English, proud to be English as well. Why wouldn't I be proud to be English? I was born in this country. It's given me a lot of opportunities. It's given me a lot of hard times and stress. But this is where I was born, I can't get away from that. I was very proud to play for England, and I wasn't afraid of the negative comments I got from being English. From white people saying 'You're not English,' from Black people saying 'You've sold out.' It didn't bother me at all. When I started doing the telly and England were on and I'd get very excited about it, people would say, 'Oh, look at Ian Wright, he's jingoistic.' Other people would call you 'Uncle Tom' or this and that. I think it was because I put myself in the situation of playing at that time, and it was very exciting.
>
> If you look at the current English football side, and you look at the [white] guys involved in it – Jack Grealish, Phil Foden, Declan Rice, James Maddison – they are so in with the Black culture. I would love England, especially in these times, with the amount of mixed-race and Black players involved with England now … nothing would make me happier than

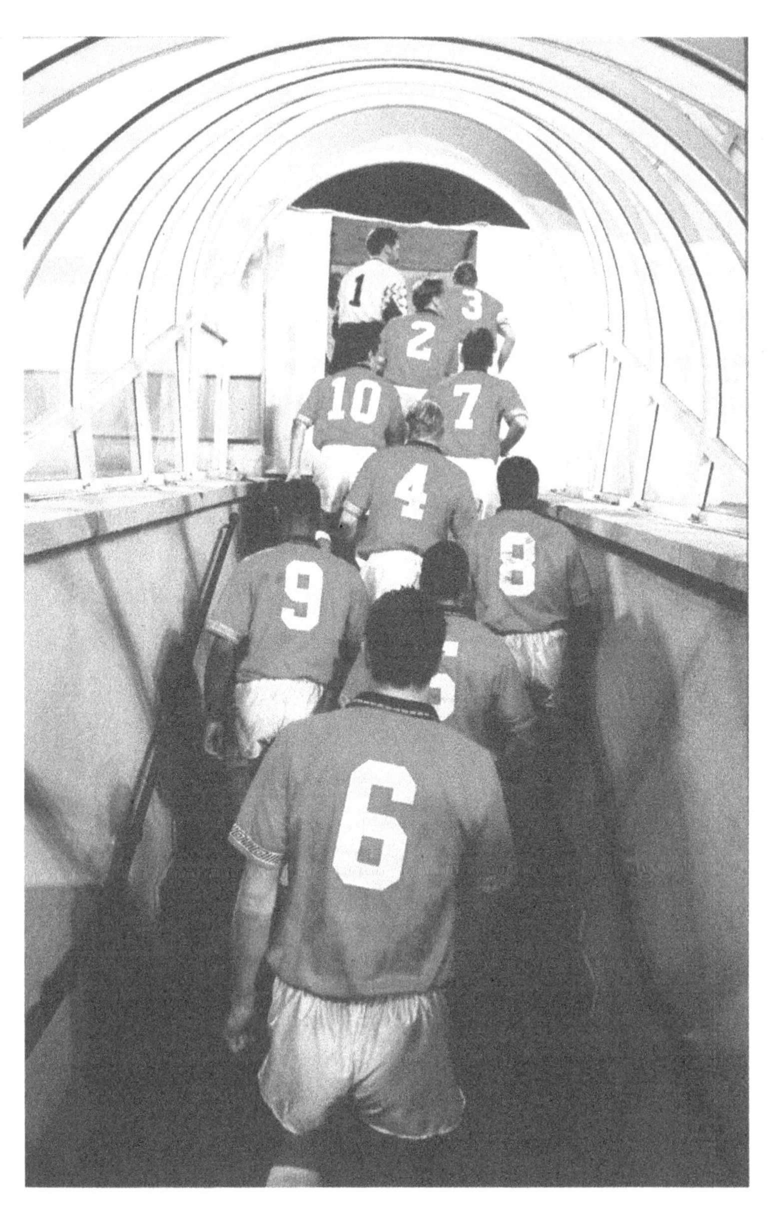

'Yes, my heritage is Jamaica, but I'm England. People for some reason can't put it together that you're Black and English, proud to be English as well.'

England winning something with this generation. There's not a better generation to represent England.

Ian Wright never made an England squad for a major tournament. The closest he came was England's failed attempt to qualify for the 1994 World Cup: a 7–1 victory in San Marino, which Graham Taylor's England needed to win by seven clear goals, while hoping that Poland defeated the Netherlands in a simultaneous tie – a result which didn't go England's way. Wright scored four of his nine England goals that day. Paul Ince scored two, and Les Ferdinand provided the other one. Celebrations from these players of Jamaican, Barbadian and Saint Lucian heritage were muted: sprinting back to the centre circle, the ball tucked in the armpit of their red away shirts, racing against the clock, battling to get their country to the tournament in the USA. Just as our elder relatives undergo hardship to make life a little easier for us, Sir Les, The Guv'nor and Uncle Ian, valiantly leading the charge, laying the foundations, the shape of football to come.

//

As well as having to figure out how to cope without structure, retirement forces footballers to rethink the metrics by which they assess their own value. At fifty-seven, Ian Wright might have taken the long way round, but in recent years he's managed to find a prominent position in the world after professional football, a position from which he can add value and contribute to the careers of young athletes. Whether on *Match of the Day*, covering an England game, through his podcast *Wrighty's House*, or through more informal pastoral care, he still buzzes with an energy for the game that's given him so much:

> When I left football, success was winning the league, winning the FA Cup, playing at Wembley, playing for England, getting the MBE and meeting the Queen. Of course I wanted to play in a World Cup, and get to a World Cup Final and stuff, but you can't have everything, and when I stopped playing I was very satisfied with what I'd done. Today, I'm not particularly worried about what Black people say [about me], or what white people say, but I think the general consensus is, 'Yeah, he's alright, he works hard, he tells the truth, speaks his mind.' That's how I judge success now.

Wright's straight-talking description of his achievements might be true to character, but he's underselling himself. I last saw Wright in person at a Football Beyond Borders event in early 2020. Invited as keynote speaker, Wright was stopped for photographs as he moved through the crowd. A white father and son posed either side of Wright. The father standing beside a goalscoring hero, the son beside a famous pundit. Two careers, with unlikely paths and a few missteps, which have ultimately resulted in success.

To my own father, Wright's achievements resonate more deeply. He represents not just a footballing icon but a Black person who's navigated life on his own terms. Besides football, the NBA, hip hop, jazz, reggae, blues, funk and their various musical offshoots, there aren't too many arenas where lots of visible Black people can achieve success.

'Being able to go back into the culture and help as much as I can is vitally important now,' Wright told me. 'I can shine a light on stuff, and things can make a massive difference.' He continued:

> I had agents who would keep me away from the community. They'd keep me away from Black causes, Black things,

> passing it on, going to schools. Now we've got prominent Black people with platforms who are able to go their own way and influence a lot of people. We're able to motorise the Black community on a global level. If you say something about Raheem Sterling, Paul Pogba, Marcus Rashford, you're going to have the world come down on you, and Black players with that kind of support can make a difference. There's a whole different structure now and it's only going to get better and better. It's very exciting.

As Wright warns young footballers, careers fly by fast, and maybe some of Wright's emotional availability is a consequence of life catching up with him. He's realising the magnitude of what he's experienced and, like Trevor McDonald, is keen to pass it on.

//

'Ethnic minority' is a sometimes troubling demographic designation, but it also speaks to an individual's reality. As we move through life in Britain, we're often placed in new and unfamiliar situations: Wright in football and television, my grandparents in London in the 1950s, my father in the 1980s after joining the Metropolitan Police, my aunt in the 1990s at university and working in finance, me in London's creative industries, my mixed-race cousin and her white husband whose three young children each have different skin tones. Again and again, it's all unprecedented.

Ian Wright is relatable not just because of the way he speaks and behaves, but because of the nature of his journey. He is proof to us all that you can be unprecedented and you can be yourself and – if you're prepared to be patient – you can be successful.

I don't mean to depict Wright as a martyr – the man who died so Ainsley Maitland-Niles and Big Narstie could live – but he came through in an era when he had to improvise and often work things out for himself. When dismissed as too small or too Sunday League, or criticised by Michael Parkinson for his early presenting skills, or when former Labour Minister for Sport Kate Hoey questioned the decision to award Wright an MBE because of his on-pitch disciplinary record, Wright had to prove people wrong. Like all of us, he's had to piece things together and work things out.

Wright's views aren't always neat. He'll talk about championing Black causes in response to one question, then in the next he'll talk about bingeing on *The Crown* and how much he loves the Queen. But that's exactly what makes him all the more real – it's the same royalism seated beside Black pride that I tease my grandparents about. Wright's spent three and a half decades at the vanguard of Black British popular culture, a hybrid culture – bogling after scoring, belting out the national anthem. And, in doing so, he helped create an England that Maitland-Niles or Saka can play for, and somebody like me can support. He's also redrawn the template for what a retired footballer can offer and achieve. He seems genuinely happy and is prepared to pass on the torch. After speaking to him, I feel like I could run through a wall. Without him, nothing in this book would be possible.

'I'm looking forward to the book,' Wright said as we wrapped up our conversation:

> It's the kind of thing that needs to happen more, and this is what I'm saying. It's about shining a light on all of us, as Black people, this is our time to shine. You'll get the white people who are like, 'Fucking hell, here we go again,' 'Oh

god, there's another Black,' [or] 'Oh they're only on there because they're Black' – this and that. It doesn't matter what those people think and it doesn't matter how we've got to this juncture, for people like yourself, for Musa, for Jeanette,* for me, for Sterling, for Rashford, for Black people to shine. It's your time. This is going to be a time of prominence, and in years to come, this time is going to be the platform from which a lot of things have risen, I'm telling you. I'm looking forward to it.

* Musa Okwonga and Jeanette Kwakye, two of the other contributors to this book.

ANDREW COLE

I Did It My Way

Calum Jacobs

Before the Conservative government-led criminality of 2018 malformed its popular conception, the word 'Windrush' used to instantly summon to mind black-and-white newsreel footage of immaculately attired Black men, drawn from all corners of the Caribbean, congregated on the decks of HMT *Empire Windrush* as she arrived at her final destination, the Tilbury Docks, in June 1948. The footage – which historian and author Kennetta Perry argues 'served as the primary point of entry for understanding the formation of postcolonial Black Britain'[1] – underscores the economic imperative that prompted these men to cross the ocean in search of opportunity in post-war Britain, ethnicising the nation in the process.

Perhaps the most widely consumed clip was produced by British Pathé. Titled *Pathé Reporter Meets Jamaicans Come to Britain to Look for Work*,[2] it begins with customarily plummy narration over shots of the ship's intrepid passengers. 'In Jamaica they couldn't find work' – why their country languished in economic depression is, of course, unexplored – 'Discouraged, but full of hope, they sailed for Britain ... many are to be found jobs. Our reporter asks them what they want to do.' Before calypso star Lord Kitchener is plucked from the crowd by the reporter to serenade the camera with his now-iconic song 'London Is the Place for Me', two men are asked why they've come to Britain. In soft, lilting accents, their voices hinting at nervousness, they shed light on some of the reasons for migration:

> Reporter: Now, why have you come to England?
> First man: To seek a job.
> Reporter: And what kind of job do you want?
> First man: Any type, so long as I get a good pay.

'Some will go into industry,' the narrator tells us. 'Others intend to re-join the services.'

> Reporter: Now, you're ex-Air Force, aren't you?
> Second man: Yes
> Reporter: Are you going back into the Air Force again? Do you know if you'll be accepted?
> Second man: I, I think so.

These responses accord with the findings of R B Davison, a former researcher at the University of the West Indies who is credited with coining the descriptor 'Black British'. For his 1962 book *West Indian Migrants: Social and Economic Facts of Migration From the West Indies*, Davison created a sample survey of West Indian migrants that sought to clearly establish their primary reason for journeying to Britain. The respondents 'answered almost unanimously "to seek employment"'.[3]

By their very nature, dominant narratives – especially those collectively romanticised to the point of near-mythology – occlude and silence accounts that don't quite align with them. These discarded stories often remain secreted in family histories beyond the walls of formal archives. It is here we find the story of Lincoln Cole, who left a life of cutting cane under the Jamaican sun, not for work, but for love. 'My dad came after my mum,' confirmed his son, Andrew Cole, when I spoke to him in August 2020. 'My mum came with her dad, my grandad, to work ... So that's why my dad ended up coming to England – cos my mum was there. My mum obviously was the woman my dad wanted to be with. So he cut from Jamaica and followed to England.'

Within hours of disembarking, the passengers of HMT *Empire Windrush* would discover that the vast majority of English people fundamentally considered their presence a problem. They were subjected to extreme discrimination in virtually every area of public life by their new hosts, who could not conceive of them as fellow citizens, irrespective of what their passports stated. This traumatic revelation represented a cruel irony for the West Indian migrants, who had been indoctrinated in all things British since the first day they sat behind a school desk. As Indian historian Dilip Hiro outlines in *Black British, White British*, 'The educational, religious and cultural centre of West Indian society lay not within itself, geographically or otherwise, but outside – in England. For the individual West Indian, coming to England was thus an inward movement. A journey into the cultural womb.'[4]

Lincoln Cole experienced this unravelling of a mis-sold dream first-hand when he arrived in England in 1957. Like many West Indian émigrés, he landed alone in a country at once alien and familiar, with the address of an earlier settler. Andrew picked up the thread:

> My dad said to me, he said he come wearing a short-sleeved shirt – I dunno where he's going in his short-sleeved shirt, only God knows. He comes, he's been given an address by someone. He went to the address, he had his case, knocked the door, a woman answered, she said, 'Ah, such and such is

Andrew Cole prepares to give an interview after Manchester United's 2–0 victory over South Melbourne at the FIFA Club World Championships in Rio De Janeiro in 2000.

not here ... No. You can't come in, but you can leave your suitcase.' So he had to leave his suitcase and then go and sit down somewhere to try and keep himself warm.

'Them kinda tings, those kinda tings stick in the back of my mind,' Andrew admitted. The quiet indignities endured by his dad burrowed themselves into Andrew's subconscious, shaping the way he related to others – including managers, coaches and teammates – but also to himself, throughout his long, successful career. Speaking to footballer-turned-psychotherapist Richie Sadlier on Second Captains podcast *The Player's Chair*, Cole repeated a phrase – 'My dad did my hard yards' – that begins to build a kind of cultural continuity between his life and that of his father, even as it marks a divergence in their experiences.[5]

Lincoln was a miner for twenty-two years. 'And that's hard work, you know,' Andrew said. 'But what we've got to accept and understand is that parents coming from the Caribbean weren't scared of hard work.' For Black parents of Lincoln's generation, labouring on behalf of their children encompassed not only provision, but protection from the threat white Britain imagined in their offsprings' dark skin. 'You cannot honestly understand what my parents' generation got when they came here,' Cole continued:

> It wasn't no bed of roses and hugs and kisses and welcome. Nah, nah. Forget that. So when I said my dad done all the hard yards for me, and my mum, you know. It's basically taking all the violent abuse, you know, trying to shield not just me, but my brother, my sisters, from what they've been through. That's hard work because I've only really spoken to my dad about it once, what you done, what you took. Nah ... nah.

The racism that defined the collective experience of the Windrush generation was exacerbated by a lack of agency. The work they found and accepted – and, by extension, the locations they settled in – were rarely a matter of choice. And so it was that Lincoln would depart London for Birmingham, before eventually settling in Lenton, Nottingham. 'Ultimately he would have stayed in London if there was work,' said Andrew. 'But all the work in London had gone. And that's when you see everyone start to branch out – you can go further south, or Midlands, or you go further up north. By the time you realise, that's where you end up living, you raise your family—' His voice drifts, and you sense he's contemplating how exposing and fundamentally unjust this migratory pattern was. 'The Windrush generation ... it's frightening how everyone spread out due to work.'

An awareness of these sacrifices, and the constant need to protect and shield from the prevalent forces of anti-Black racism were background music throughout Andrew's childhood. The volume increased when he decided to enter into the sifting process aspiring young footballers begin in an attempt to reach the hallowed grounds of Lilleshall, the FA's now-defunct school of footballing excellence. Father and son had already clashed over Andrew's obsession with a sport that, in the early 1980s, was a cultural product associated almost entirely with the so-called 'white working class'. Although Andrew's mother attempted to understand her son's desire to become a footballer, Lincoln had no such intentions. 'My dad fought from the opposite corner,' Cole wrote in his eponymous autobiography, published in 1999. 'He was aggressive, as I saw it then, authoritarian and hellbent on getting me back in line. He used to bark at me: "I sent you to school to get an education – not just to play football." He was very much a disciplinarian and typical of his Caribbean upbringing.'[6]

Alongside the cultural incompatibilities between cricket-loving West Indian parents and football, Lincoln feared that the game would prove too hostile a domain for a Black man. Writ large in his actions was an urge, again, to protect. So, even when the single-minded and singularly brilliant Andrew beat off thousands of young footballers through the Midlands 'eliminators' and became one of the select handful admitted to Lilleshall, Lincoln remained apprehensive.

'To a certain extent everyone – no, not to a certain extent, *everyone* – was positive and everyone wanted me to do the right thing. With my dad … it was different with my dad,' Cole said.

> But it's only now, I'm at the age now, I understand the reasons why. When I was younger, I didn't understand the reasons why, but as you grow older, you realise your parents want to keep you out of harm's way. I thought, when my dad was telling me about football, that I 'couldn't play football'. You know, the reason being, 'You're Black, and you will not be accepted, as being Black, and if you do football you have to accept you are gonna have to be twice, if not three times better than your white counterpart.' At the time, I said to my dad, 'You're talking nonsense, I'm not having it.' But I'm a grown man now, and I understand exactly what he was saying. But it's taken me to be a grown man to actually understand what I've been through, to say, you know what, 'My dad was right from the start,' because those were his experiences.

Thus, whether as a figure to rebel against, his life an exemplar of the prescribed racial fate that Andrew refused, or as a barometer for the behaviour Andrew would accept from coaches ('A lot of the time they tried to talk to me too hard; I'd say "Uh uh. My dad can't talk to me like that, so stop it"'), Lincoln was an overarching influence on his son's life. Today, advice Lincoln dispensed decades ago continues to operate as a compass orienting Cole in the present. Life since retirement hasn't been kind to Andrew. His well-documented kidney disease – he received a transplant from his nephew,

Alexander – has the potential to debilitate him for days at a time. He has subsequently battled depression, which he publicly described as 'torture'. But, ultimately, he now understands himself far better than he did as a reserved young footballer.

During his football career, Cole's relationship with the media became so strained that he eventually avoided interacting with them altogether, which in turn allowed them to perpetuate a distorted image of him. As a result, to write about him now feels like a historical correction. Although painted by the press as a difficult interviewee, Cole is actually a classic introvert, a quiet, self-contained individual who eschews attention. Yet he also has a distinct and deep pride in his Blackness. 'I'm very proud. I'm a very proud Black man,' Cole said. 'The way people try and talk to me, the way they try and talk to people of colour – I can't accept.' This combination proved incomprehensible to the almost exclusively white football press, who were unable to orient their analyses through a lens that differed from their own experiences.

Cole's perspective was intrinsically shaped by the political and sociocultural climate of the 1970s, the decade in which he was born, and a moment that shaped a generation of Black people who were 'here to stay' and redefined how they understood themselves and their place in society. This formative moment in the construction of the personal and political identity of Black people in Britain was influenced by the culture-led self-definition that moved across the wider African diaspora in the late 1960s and early 1970s. At this point, the children of the Windrush generation felt like outsiders in the country of their birth. Wider society remained as alien, cold and closed off to them as it did to their parents, and, as a result of persistent racism, Black people were three times more likely to be unemployed than whites during the economic recession of 1973–75.

Confronted by the seeming impossibility of cultivating a future on inhospitable English soil, Black British youths sought identification, warmth and sanctuary in house parties and Black social clubs found in church halls and community centres. At the same time, pop-culture icons, such as a defiant Muhammad Ali, Shaft and Michael Jackson, were beamed in from the USA. The result was an unapologetic Black British identity visually defined by afros, platform shoes and flares.

The pioneering figure of Bob Marley, who was first introduced to Britain on BBC Two's music show *The Old Grey Whistle Test*, also played a central role in the formation of this emerging culture. Where Ali and Jackson built communion between Black Britons and African-Americans, Marley's lyrics helped them to map their features onto Jamaica and, through Rastafarianism, the continent of Africa. Though his presence would soon pervade the mainstream, Marley's initial impact was upon Black youth. Simultaneously representing salvation and political defiance, Marley's music and aesthetic offered them strength in the face of marginalisation, and succinctly encapsulated the feelings of a generation beginning to conceive of the Black experience as globally interconnected.

As cultural theorist and public intellectual Stuart Hall explained in the 2001 BBC Four documentary *Windrush: A New Generation*,[7] Bob Marley's cultural intervention was existentially life-saving for Black British identity:

> It's conjured out of the back end of the Bible, the Bible read upside down, you know, myths about Haile Selassie ... It's conjured out the boogie box that plays roots reggae music, you know, it's conjured out of stories coming out of Kingston – the gun court and Trench Town – it's conjured out of scraps, really. Bits and pieces. But they manufacture

> for themselves a Black identity that they feel proud of ... And my honest opinion to you is that that generation would have committed a kind of collective social suicide without the birth of that kind of Black British identity.

On the same documentary, Jamaican dub poet Linton Kwesi Johnson outlined the transformative attitudinal shift that resulted in second-generation immigrant children. 'We didn't have the kinds of constraints that our parents had,' he explained from behind dark glasses. He continued:

> They had mortgages to pay, they had to put you to school, they had to find food, and when the foreman in the factory called dem a 'black bastard', sometimes, even if you didn't like it, you would have to put up with it. My generation didn't have to put up with it – and we didn't.

The consequences of this generational shift were seismic. As the children of the Windrush generation came of age, they embraced a non-conformist spirit that brought an end to the blanket acceptance of the assimilationist dream that their socially conservative parents had urged them to adhere to. They would no longer prioritise the feelings of white Britain by altering their appearances, changing their names or concealing their culture. Unlike their parents, they understood that to live 'removed from oneself' – in the words of the Trinidadian author V S Naipaul – was no guard against the pervasive tentacles of anti-Black racism.

In *Black Britain: A Photographic History*, Paul Gilroy argued that this generation's militancy, their boldness and their reckless despair were forces that would eventually bring about the ambivalent mainstreaming of Black culture in Britain.[8] A special daring, shaped above all by hopelessness, was what generated the tides of protest that eventually birthed a small Black British middle-class buoyed up by tokenism and firmly anchored in the world of entertainment media and local government politics.

This was the shifting demographic and cultural milieu into which Andrew Cole was born.

When his early years are situated in this context, what followed feels inevitable, for, while all these tectonic shifts were reshaping the wider world, they did not make a dent in the hermetically sealed football industry. By its design, the football industry disbarred insubordination. Overt political activity of any kind was not tolerated by its governing bodies, and authority was ultimately determined by managers and the white, hyper-masculine governance of the changing room. To oppose this state of affairs amounted to near-certain career suicide. The increasing player power we are witnessing across sport today was an alien concept.

The template of how to navigate this restrictive arena with dignity and composure was provided by the late, great Cyrille Regis, who made his debut for West Bromwich Albion in 1977. Through his behaviour and achievements, he showed aspiring Black footballers and the smattering of fellow Black players at other clubs at the time that, although confronting the pervasive racist ideologies which gripped the game head on was ill-advised, they didn't have to be entirely subservient. The task was to rise above it.

Like almost all Black strikers drawn from his generation, Andrew Cole idolised Regis. But he understood, even as a child, that he could not emulate Regis's approach to the white-hot hostility that awaited him:

> Growing up, my idol, my pioneer, for me, was Cyrille Regis. I just loved the way he conducted himself. I loved the way,

> you know, he dealt with things ... And I used to say to myself, if I could ever be like that, I mean, I would try my best to be like that but ... that ain't me, if you feel what I'm saying. That ain't me.

Whereas football could accept the dignity and stoicism of Regis – who, through his on- and off-pitch behaviour, increased tolerance for Black players among white fans – the terraces, and even the clubs themselves, were less keen on those they couldn't explicitly categorise or command. Managers, coaches and senior players saw it as part of their remit to create subordinates, resorting to crude psychological means to control those who wouldn't play their assigned part. Cole would not yield to this, and neither was he interested in currying favour. These things simply weren't part of his make-up. 'It's a case of tryna keep people onside, convincing them to like you,' Cole explained to me:

> So, they can say, 'Oh yeah, he's a nice kid this one.' But what you've gotta realise is people don't like people who are quiet, because how do you categorise someone like that? People don't like that. In football they don't like it ... they wanna mentally get into your head and deal with ya. So, when I was younger, I heard a lot of people say, 'Don't worry about it. I'll get into his head, I'll be able to deal with him.' I used to laugh. I had to laugh, cos I used to turn around and say 'Yeah? I can't get into my own head, so I know you're fucked.'

As a footballer, Andrew Cole was built to bear the physical and mental toll of performing at the pinnacle of the sport, but off the field he simply wasn't. Cole, a shy but proud product of the 1970s Black cultural awakening, jarred with the hegemonic white world of football. This incompatibility was the animus for many of Cole's well-documented fallouts with coaches, which are now the stuff of footballing folklore. But to explore Cole's story only through this binary is to eliminate a layer of complexity from the narrative. The fact is that he was, on occasion, an exceptionally difficult boy and man – sometimes unnecessarily, as Cole himself is quick to acknowledge:

> My auntie always used to say, 'Bwoy, your head hard you know.' My mum used to say mad times, 'Andrew stop it, please.' I remember, I used to go away and play football, and you know when you've got the white kids, and their parents would say, 'Go and have a lovely time, enjoy it,' and whatever. My mum used to say to me, 'Please behave, Andrew, please behave yourself.' So, I said, 'Aite, Mum, of course.' 'Please, I'm begging ya, just behave yaself.'
>
> I know where I've come from. I know how difficult it is, but at the same time, I'm making it harder for myself, because I'm not accepting nuttem from nobody. I mean, I'm on the edge, I'm always on the edge ... and that's what I was like from when I was fourteen up to possibly twenty-three, twenty-four ... I'm not accepting no nonsense.

Thus, when he was pushed to breaking point, the blame didn't always lie solely with coaches who held racist views about Black people. Sometimes he snapped because of his own inflexibility.

As Cole recalled in his biography the disharmony that pockmarked his early career began at his hometown club, Nottingham Forest, when he played for a junior side. After a training session, he re-entered the dressing room to be met by Peter Davenport, Forest's star striker at the time, and Liam

O'Kane, a youth team coach charged with the protection of kids like Cole. 'Hey Chalky', Davenport said, 'can you go and do this job for me?' As O'Kane laughed his head off, Cole turned to Davenport and calmly replied, 'Nah, that's not for me, not the way you talk.'[9] Cole quit on the spot.

Given his long association with Manchester United, images of Cole in Arsenal kit – Cole was briefly signed to the Gunners at the beginning of his professional career back in 1989 – are almost surreal. It's strange to think that Cole, rather than Ian Wright, could have been the iconic Black British striker fondly remembered by Gunners supporters. However, manager George Graham and assistant manager Pat Rice ensured that this possibility never came to be, as Cole wrote in his autobiography:

> All that was needed for someone to ease down on the detonator. That person turned out to be Rice. He kept chivvying, needling and having a go at me in training. I couldn't control my emotions any longer and I snapped. There was a whole salvo of effing and blinding, then I snarled at him, 'I'm off, that's me finished here,' and I stormed off the park.[10]

After hurriedly packing his bags at his girlfriend Shirley's house, Cole caught a train back to his family home in Nottingham the same day. His parents couldn't believe he was about to torch his dreams, and talked him into returning to London to reconcile with Rice and the club. Though he followed their advice, he felt his card had been blotted, and that his opportunities would be thwarted. Nineteen-year-old Cole asked for an audience with Graham, at which he outlined, quite plainly, that he deserved to be on the team. Graham told him he had a 'chip on his shoulder' and a 'bad attitude'.[11] The meeting signalled the end of Cole's career at Arsenal.

'A lot of people suggest now that I was too abrasive, too argumentative, and too arrogant for Graham in my early years,' Cole wrote. 'It wasn't that at all – it was simply a case of being seriously committed to my ambition and having great self-belief to make certain that the dream eventually came true.'[12] Graham, who then-Arsenal captain Tony Adams dubbed 'Colonel Gaddafi', was the type of abrasive disciplinarian that has now been almost entirely purged from the game. In view of Cole's description of his temperament and psyche at that time, it's unsurprising that the two had such an explosive dynamic.

Ian Wright and Cole's paths crossed briefly at Arsenal. On his podcast, *Wrighty's House*,[13] in October 2020, Wright revealed that Cole was correct in assuming the coaching staff disliked him:

> They said about Andrew Cole, 'No, he's never gonna score more than ten goals because he's lazy.' They would talk about his attitude and stuff ... They'd say, 'He is someone special, [but] I don't think he's gonna get it in time.' And I remember watching him in the games and it would be very easy for people like the coaches and that to say, 'Nah, move him on to someone else,' because when he was doing the running [in training] he was like thirty or forty yards behind other people. But when he played in games you would see he'd *do* something, but you've seen that player cast aside so many times.

What Cole really needed was an arm around the shoulder and some encouraging words. He would find these things – via a loan move to Fulham, where he had another falling out, this time with Jimmy Hill, and a prolific stint at Bristol City – at Newcastle, with Kevin Keegan. It was there that Cole would announce his lethality to the world, hauling the club into the Premiership in the process. Over three blistering seasons, he racked up a ludicrous sixty-eight goals in eighty-four appearances, and became the fastest ever player to score fifty goals in Premier League history.

Under the loose and warm instruction of Keegan – who'd tracked Cole's progress at Bristol City and rung him personally to propose the move up north – Cole was finally thriving in exactly the type of environment Arsenal had been unable to provide. Keegan's confidence and investment of value in Cole were absolute. He took Cole on random scouting trips to ask his opinion about which defenders to buy. He also signed Peter Beardsley to

Over three blistering seasons at Newcastle, Andrew Cole racked up a ludicrous sixty-eight goals in eighty-four appearances to become the fastest ever player to score fifty goals in Premier League history.

play just behind him. This totally confounded Cole: 'What did he mean … trying to buy a player for me, just for me?'[14]

Cole's rich goalscoring form also meant that he was rapidly adopted as a hero by the Newcastle natives, but he couldn't bear the resulting adulation. He also felt profoundly isolated in the Victorian house he rented in Crook, a small mining village outside Newcastle, an echo of the distinct flavour of alienation experienced by the Windrush generation as they spread out across Britain.

As sure as night follows day, Cole fell out with Keegan too. Having witnessed his good friend and Newcastle teammate Lee Clark reprimanded by Keegan during a match at Southampton, the next day, Cole, in a warped attempt to show solidarity, told Keegan that he 'didn't fancy' training. This resulted in a row that caused Keegan to tell Cole to 'eff off' – a term Lincoln would never have thrown at him. And so, Cole hurtled once more along the motorway, this time back to London and to Shirley. Cole's agent, Paul Stretford (a name now more associated with Wayne Rooney), and his family eventually talked him round, and after a mediation session in the home of former Newcastle chairman Freddy Shepherd, he returned to Newcastle. This period illustrates a character trait that Cole now knows worked to his detriment:

> My stubbornness is my biggest strength, but also my biggest weakness. I will end up fighting myself knowing that I shouldn't fight myself … And then the penny actually drops, and I think, 'Nah, nah, you shouldn't have done that.' But it's too late now … So all the decisions I made back when I was younger, I turn round and say to myself, 'Man, I didn't even know I was that bad' – and it's only about a year ago I realised just how bad I was when I was younger.

Although Keegan quickly forgave Cole, a subtle strain was introduced to their relationship. By 1995, with Newcastle's attacking patterns becoming too predictable, Keegan sought to evolve the team to make it less dependent on Cole. And so, in the midwinter he sold Cole – without consulting him – to the only English club he would have countenanced moving to: Manchester United.

The £7 million deal – at the time a British record – stunned the football world. Visibly distraught Newcastle fans congregated on the steps of St James' Park as a mulleted Kevin Keegan faced them down. However, nobody was more spun by it than Andrew Cole. 'It wasn't that I didn't wish to join Manchester United,' he wrote. 'No, that wasn't exactly the feeling. I was just bewildered by the speed of it all. Earlier that same day I had had no concept of moving away from Newcastle; now I had been sold, sealed and almost delivered without having a say in the whole business.'[15]

Wearing a black pinstripe suit, his handsome features softened by the dull grain of the Sky Sports footage that captured the press conference on the day of his signing, Cole looks slightly lost, almost overwhelmed by the situation he finds himself at the centre of. But the defensive, combative edge remained. As his eyes shift around the press room, a journalist asks if he's shocked. 'It's a big shock,' he fires back almost immediately. 'It's a big shock to you boys as well, cos no one thought that Kevin Keegan would sell me to arch-rivals Man United, but I'm just looking forward to it.'

Yet for the first eighteen months of his career at Manchester United, Cole struggled. Badly. The record fee weighed heavily on the shoulders of the 23-year-old, as did the pressure of meeting the specific demands of playing for a super club. In both games and training, he began to try too hard, verbally persecuting himself for mistakes in front of his teammates. The experience took a toll on his mental health. His response was typical of an introverted, prideful Black man. He shut people out. Sequestered away in Stretford's home, he became something of a hermit. Per his autobiography: 'I became Fortress Cole for a while, barricaded and shuttered against the world. Nobody really got close to me in that period. In doing that I made the whole experience a lot tougher than it should have been.'[16]

Here, another parallel between a stoic Jamaican father and his son emerges. 'I'm a typical man,' said Cole during his appearance on *The Player's Chair*. 'A typical man always suppresses, always suppresses his feelings. I think even more so from my heritage as well. Caribbean men always suppress their feelings – they'll hold it and hold it, and oftentimes they'll take it to their grave.' Cole also revealed that his dad effectively buried the trauma he carries as a result of moving to England so deeply that it's only surfaced in conversation once, a fact that he also confirmed to me.

It seldom got any easier for Cole. When you consider the trials he faced and headed off, the fact he succeeded at all feels almost unrealistic. Whether owing to injury, form or incessant tabloid scrutiny, at the outset of each of his first three seasons at Manchester United he had to prove himself anew. After two seasons of what amounted to middling form, in the summer of 1996, United were linked with then-England captain, Alan Shearer. But in a *Sliding Doors*-esque turn of events, the transfer collapsed, and Shearer moved to Newcastle instead. Cole realised at this moment it was make or break for him – he couldn't afford another flawed campaign. What happened next is scarcely believable: he contracted pneumonia and broke his ankle. Then, in early October, having overcome these setbacks, his leg was deliberately broken by Neil Ruddock in a reserve game, costing him another five months out. By the end of the 1996–97 season, Cole had just eleven goals to his name. Relief of sorts arrived in 1997, as Cole plundered twenty-five goals across all competitions. However, never content, United manager Alex Ferguson sought to sharpen United's attacking prowess further by attempting to sign Patrick Kluivert, a different type of striker, from AC Milan in 1998.

As Cole tells it, had United signed Kluivert, he would have been moved on as part of the ruthless squad churn Ferguson was famed for. However, this widely accepted story lacks nuance: Kluivert never had any intention of joining Manchester United. Wearing a white baseball cap backwards, he dismissively told ITV sports reporter Gabriel Clarke that there was nothing to the link: 'For me, at that moment there was only one club in England, and that's Arsenal.' He even refused to meet Ferguson to talk.

At this point, Ferguson switched his attention to signing the best striker in the domestic league: Aston Villa's Dwight Yorke. Indeed, this would become something of a pattern for Ferguson – after first Cole, and then Yorke, he would later sign Saha, Rooney, Berbatov and van Persie. The sudden acquisition of Yorke led Cole to worry that his opportunities would soon be limited, and initially that seemed to be the case. The threat to Cole didn't come from Yorke himself, though – rather, it came from Ferguson's strategic approach.

After testing the two together in a game at West Ham, Cole was substituted after seventy minutes. This felt ominous, and appeared to signal the beginning of his being side-lined. For the next two months, Cole became a glorified substitute. Feeling like a spare part, and as if his time at Manchester United once again seemed to be drawing to a conclusion, he sat down with Ferguson to try to understand his manager's reasoning. 'I don't think it is working out. I have yet to be convinced there is a partnership there to build on with you and Dwight,' is what Cole wrote Ferguson told him. 'I can't see you two doing it, so I have got to look at my options.'[17]

While the conversation watered the roots of Cole's latent insecurities, Ferguson assured him he would still get his chances. And, true to his word, after a testing Champions League tie away to Bayern Munich, Ferguson swapped out Teddy Sheringham for Cole for an away game at Southampton. United ran out easy 3–0 victors, with Yorke and Cole bagging a goal each. 'That was the real christening of the partnership with Yorke, which subsequently delivered fifty-three goals over the following mid-winter months,' is how Cole would describe it whenever asked in the proceeding years.

Any analysis of Cole and Yorke's on-pitch partnership must be informed by their off-pitch relationship – their friendship and rich form are intrinsically linked. From the outset, despite believing that he was being usurped, Cole went out of his way to help Yorke feel welcome and settled. He did this in large part because of the social isolation he felt at Newcastle. 'I remembered my own isolation, the life of the hermit, and I didn't want anyone else to suffer the same way. I realised I could help him settle in very quickly,' Cole wrote.[18] The fact Yorke was Black played a 'massive part' in this behaviour. His parents' influence was also significant, he told me:

> I gotta be honest, my parents have brought me up the right way, you know? I ain't here to begrudge nobody, it's as simple as that. If a man can play ball better than me, he can play ball better than me. I ain't gonna begrudge you. If you're bringing suttem to the party, you're bringing suttem to the party. So with me and Yorkie, naturally I'm gonna gravitate

> towards him cos he's another Black man as well. We have the same heritage – different islands, but the same heritage. But I wanted to bring him in and make him comfortable, quickly make him as comfortable as possible. Because Man United is no normal football club. So he comes in. And yeah, I go out my way, but I easily go out my way cos that's me. I'm just a positive individual when it comes to those kind of things, I'm not a grudgeful guy. My mum and my sister brought me up to be better than that. So with Yorkie, it's just a case of 'Bruv, come in, I wanna try and help you settle as quickly as possible.' Even if I'm not gonna be here, I can look at myself and say, 'You know what, I tried my best to help the brother when he first came to the club.'

Cole's actions, which sit on a continuum that began at the inception of Black British identity in 1948, recall those of Moses Aloetta, the chief protagonist and moral centre of Sam Selvon's *The Lonely Londoners* – perhaps the most audacious Caribbean novel ever written. Aloetta, an early-settler in London from Trinidad, has lived in the 'metropole' for several years and operates as an official welfare officer to newer arrivals, inducting them into English customs, helping them to find accommodation in appropriate areas and securing them employment where possible. Each introduced character – all of whom are Black men – operates as an anthropological investigator, turning their gaze upon the peculiarities of Englishness. While they all experience the city differently, every character is haunted by loneliness, isolation and anonymity. Aloetta understands that communion is a precondition for their collective survival and, although seemingly reluctant, welcomes the assortment of Black men into his small rented room: 'This is a lonely miserable city, if it was that we didn't get together now and then to talk about things back home, we would suffer like hell.'[19]

Today, many dressing rooms are, in a cultural sense, dominated – creolised even – by Black players. We hear that they take charge of music selections, introduce slang to their white teammates and generally act as a font from which joy flows. But just two decades ago, this wasn't the case. Cole's building with Yorke of a micro-Black community within the dressing room was of vital importance at a time when the opportunity for relation along lines of shared heritage remained slim. There is a precedent for the importance of this type of relationship in the football world. In *Pitch Black*, Emy Onuora details the influence that Laurie Cunningham had on Cole's hero, Cyrille Regis, at West Bromwich Albion, when he signed with the club in 1977. 'It was great having him around,' Regis said:

> He kind of took me under his wing, and we became friends almost immediately. It was good that one of the first-team players took an interest in me and, with him being Black and from London, made it more important. I looked up to him and it's only when I think back now that me being there was as good for him as it was for me.[20]

Yorke did something similar to Cole. He softened his friend's more pointed edges and brought him out of himself, cracking open the carapace that Cole had constructed in the years prior. Cole confirmed this: 'Yeah definitely, because, you know, he's infectious, he'll bring it out of ya. Yorkie understands me. He understands what I am, he isn't, and, vice versa. Yorkie wants to be, and is, he's gotta be the life and soul of tings.' Yorke's gregariousness, his unabashed exuberance – easily identifiable

Andrew Cole and Dwight Yorke celebrate together in the changing room after Manchester United's victory over Juventus in the semi-final of the 1998–99 Champions League. Their friendship – which remains as true and deep today as it was twenty years ago – can be read as a subtle expansion of what platonic friendships can mean and contain.

via the trademark turned-up collar and near-permanent broad grin – took the burden of attention away from Cole, a scenario in which he thrives: 'I work with an individual like him cos he takes all the shine away from me, and I can just be in the background, doing my ting, and there's where I've enjoyed living my life.'

Speaking to *Match of the Day* after a regulation 5–1 drubbing of Wimbledon at Old Trafford in 1998, a match in which he grabbed a brace while Yorke scored one, Cole, standing against a backdrop of now mostly defunct sponsors (Allsports, SHARP, Sun Microsystems), is asked if he's enjoying the partnership between him and Yorke:

> I'm really enjoying it, you know – because we're good friends off the pitch, you know? He comes round me 'ouse. We talk

> all the time. He phones me in the morning and gives me a wake-up call, and things like that. So we get on really well together. We do everything together, so the partnership is doing really well on the pitch as well.

This inseparability is a pronounced feature of their friendship, which remains almost closer to an intertwining of souls. Speaking to football magazine *FourFourTwo* in 2010, Cole was not afraid to use romantic language to depict their closeness: 'When we started playing together, it was like meeting a special woman and falling in love. Everything felt right. We never had a cross word. If I was upset with him or he with me, we'd look at each other and say, "OK."'[21] He reiterated this sentiment in conversation with me, a decade later: 'I always say to people for me personally, if I found a woman like Dwight's personality, who understood me for me, that is me sorted – cos the way me and him got on, we never had a row, we never fallen out, we don't have cross words, nuffink.'

Cole's confidence in discussing their friendship in these intimate terms can be read as subtle expansion of what platonic friendships can mean and contain. Society's narrow perception of masculinity means that it still struggles to conceive of what male friendships can encompass. That Cole and Yorke's enduring relationship upends this publicly – in the hyper-masculine sporting arena – is a clear indication of how deep and true their connection remains. As bell hooks put it in *We Real Cool*, her book about masculinity and Black men, 'Black men loving Black men is a revolutionary act'.[22]

Whereas most white fans will have witnessed two men forming a friendship that fostered their famed 'telepathic understanding' on the pitch, for supporters drawn from the African diasporic community, Yorke and Cole's partnership took on much deeper significance. They saw the emblematic image of two Black men – one the son of Windrush parents, the other an import from the Caribbean – bonding on the grandest stage of all and forging a connection through their shared Blackness that defined and drove one of the most successful periods in Manchester United's contemporary history. Cole and Yorke expanded the limits of what a striking duo could comprise and achieve. Their kinship, just as much as the goals they scored, is why Cole and Yorke continue to be so revered in the African diasporic community in Britain.

During the 1998–99 season, when Manchester United dominated domestically and in Europe, playing two 'up top' was the norm, but their peers – Inzaghi and Del Piero, Salas and Vieri, Rivaldo and Kluivert, Raúl and Morientes – never came close to touching the divine communion of Yorke and Cole. Their otherworldly symbiosis was recognised by commentators, described as 'a friendship about to blossom into the perfect football marriage' by Clive Tyldesley. 'Talk about being on the same wavelength,' exclaimed Martin Tyler. 'These two are in perfect harmony.' To this day, they endure as the duo against which striking partnerships are measured.

The reasoning for this enduring legacy can be discovered in their similar physical profiles and lethal attributes. There was no 'weaker foot' you could show them on to that would reduce their threats, no angle from which they became less reluctant to attack, no part of the foot they were unwilling to use. Added to all that was a surfeit of tremendous speed, skill and world-class movement. Most importantly, they displayed an effortless synchronicity that couldn't be taught or imitated.

Among the multitude of goals they crafted and gift-wrapped for each other – many delivered at pivotal moments that altered the trajectory of matches in favour of Manchester United – a few stand out. There's the equaliser against Juventus in the semi-final of the Champions League in 1999. With the game already stretched in the first half, Cole collected the ball to the right of the D, touched it tenderly out of his feet and surveyed the penalty area. Before he could see Yorke's move, he'd sensed it, and delivered a dinked cross with enough power on it that the arriving Yorke, who'd made a ghostly run off the back of his defender, had only to meet it with his outstretched forehead, driving the ball past Angelo Peruzzi. In the FA Cup sixth-round replay against Chelsea that same year, Cole hurtled into a challenge, his ribs shuddering against Marcel Desailly's shin, so that the ball could break free, leaving Yorke open to run in and send a twenty-yard chip with the velocity of an Exocet over the stranded figure of Ed de Goey.

The goal that represents the apotheosis of Cole and Yorke's on- and off-pitch kinship came against Barcelona on 25 November 1998 at the Nou Camp. You know the one – you can summon it from your memory with ease. Paul Scholes, ten yards inside his own half, sweeps a pass across the pitch to a shaven-headed Roy Keane, who is advancing into the Barcelona half in the space Beckham made his own. Keane glances up and arrows a pass with pace and purpose into the feet of Yorke, who elaborately dummies the ball, stepping over it with his left leg, and continues his run towards the box. This manoeuvre allows Cole, who's five yards farther forward at the tip of the penalty arc, to use the pace of Keane's ball to fire a pass back into Yorke's path. Yorke instantly returns the ball to Cole, now free and just a few yards away from the penalty spot. Cole takes a touch and coolly passes the ball into the bottom of Ruud Hesp's net. In all, the move lasts six seconds. Cole's finish lives on as one of the greatest Champions

League goals of all time, encrusted by a layer of nostalgia and enshrined in digital amber on social media, treasured as a piece of collective sporting memorabilia by United fans and neutrals alike.

If there was any lingering underestimation of Cole and Yorke's individual and collective abilities, it was expunged that night. Their accomplished evisceration of the storied European giants – Europe had seldom seen such fluidity and daring – fused the duo in a way that hasn't been seen since. Pop culture recognised and built upon the significance of the moment. In Nike's iconic 2000 advert 'The Mission' – an ambitious, Hollywood-esque creative showpiece that featured a crack team of superstar footballers recruited by the then-Netherlands manager Louis van Gaal to retrieve a Nike ball from an army of robotic ninjas – Cole and Yorke appeared together. They even wore matching white tops, while everyone else wore black, to reinforce that they came as a pair.

When appraised as a duet, Yorke and Cole are remembered with reverence and affection. However, when the two are prised apart and examined as distinct individuals, the reputations of both tend to be diminished. For Cole's abilities to be down-played in this manner feels particularly pointed, given that he is indisputably the greatest Black British striker this country has ever produced. While the ever-inflating number of statistics can sometimes suck the innate joy, unpredictability and ridiculous-ness out of football, those that offer a framework of indisputable clarity will always be welcome. Here are a few that are especially edifying. Andrew Cole's tally of 187 goals means that he remains the third-highest goalscorer in Premier League history thirteen years after his retirement. After penalties are excluded from Alan Shearer's esteemed record, Cole is just sixteen goals behind him, despite playing twenty-seven fewer matches. If penalties are removed from Wayne Rooney's total, Cole sits only one goal behind him. Cole is the only player to outright top the rankings for both goals scored and assists provided in a single Premier League season, scoring thirty-four goals and laying on a further thirteen for his Newcastle teammates during the 1993–94 season.

Yet when Gary Lineker, Ian Wright and Alan Shearer convened to rank the Premier League's top goalscorers for a mid-March *Match of the Day* lockdown special in 2020, Cole was ranked only tenth. Discussions about 'who is the best' are juvenile and subjective, but to rank Cole several places below players who'd scored a third of his goals felt strange, unfair and disrespectful. Cole, understandably, was rankled:

> People still don't wanna talk about how I'm the quickest [to fifty goals]. They will talk about second, third, fourth, look at such and such. And that's what they done throughout my career, you know. You look at my goals, I've been retired coming up to twelve years now, I'm third. I'm there, black and white, and people don't wanna talk about that. I scored one penalty in the whole of my career – of 187 goals, that's 186 from open play. And people wanna dismiss that as like man's an eediat.

The explanation for this unfathomable underrating of Cole becomes clearer when you consider that he exists at the intersection of a Venn diagram of lamentable factors: white England's inability to take Black players to their hearts (a point Gary Neville explicitly made in 2018 on *Monday Night Football* when discussing Raheem Sterling as I discussed in the introduction to this book), his previous Cold War with the football media and a paradoxical preference for foreign players, who are often judged 'sexier' than British-born ones.

Cole's very public dispute with Glenn Hoddle – and by extension his dissatisfaction with the way he was used by England while at the peak of his powers – seeps into the crevices of this discussion. In *The Promised Land: Manchester United's Historic Treble*, sports writer Daniel Harris re-maps the dimensions of their feud:

> The day before England's game with the Czech Republic, Andy Cole finally voiced his vexation with Glenn Hoddle, who had left him out of the squad for that game and also for the World Cup, because he needed 'five chances before he scores'. Only a year earlier, he [Hoddle] had paid £7.5 million for Kevin Davies. 'His behaviour towards me has been cowardly,' Cole told *The Sun*. 'He is a bad communicator. His comments about me are disrespectful. Is he a man or a mouse?'[23]

Hoddle's attitude towards Cole was bizarre, even for him. His logic of measuring a goalscorer not on the goals he scores but on those he doesn't very much missed the point: Cole did miss a few chances, as all strikers do, but so many more chances came his way by virtue of the alertness, anticipation and imagination that separated him from contemporaries. Nonetheless, Hoddle selected Emile Heskey and Dion Dublin ahead of Cole. 'Dion Dublin was impeccable,' he would tell the press after the game. 'Anyone who suggested he is not an international player should be embarrassed.'[24]

After both their retirements, former Arsenal and France striker Thierry Henry told Cole that, outside of England, he was widely respected – specifically by other Black strikers who played on the continent. Henry reiterated his own admiration for Cole during an episode of Sky Sports' *Monday Night Football*. A week prior, Henry had become one of the first footballers inducted into the Premier League's Hall of Fame. After Henry is quizzed by the show's presenter, Dave Jones, about whom he would admit into the Hall of Fame alongside himself – Roy Keane, Eric Cantona, Dennis Bergkamp, Paul Scholes, Patrick Vieira and Frank Lampard, if you were interested – he was asked to say a few words about the striker he most enjoyed watching who hadn't made his six-man shortlist. "There was, you know, Nicolas Anelka, Didier Drogba, we can name them all, I would have loved to play with those guys. I did play with Nicolas for the [French] national team. But Andy Cole." To emphasise and dramatise the point he was making, Henry pauses and momentarily turns away from Jones. "Ahhh, stop it." Turning back to Jones, Henry simply repeats his name: "Andy Cole. Wow, wow, wow, wow."

When Black people look upon Cole and his work, we see something entirely different from the rest of the population. Over time, Cole has come to appreciate this acknowledgement more than the widespread recognition you sense he once craved:

> I've been very, very lucky that way. Wherever I have been, the love and respect I have got from all amounts of Black people for achieving what I've done, but doing it in a way … They look at it as, *You've done it in a way that we wanted to see you do it, you done it your way. You're not toeing the line, you're not jumping through hoops* … bun that, I ain't really business with that. So, when people say, 'He's one of us,' I don't think people understand just how proud that makes me feel.

This type of recognition doesn't begin and end with Cole. The necessity of Black people – driven by a desire to protect – holding each other close and building familial bonds with those whom they're not related to, can be charted back to the darkest period of our history. Its force and beauty make it resistant to fetishisation, commodification or ready capture. It is neither trite nor imagined. It is perhaps the most enduring aspect of the Black experience. To Black people, Andrew Cole represented defiance, self-respect and an unapologetic Blackness that many of us were not yet able to adopt openly in our places of work. His refusal to yield or compromise in the presence of the likes of George Graham or Glenn Hoddle is the foundation upon which his legend and legacy is built.

Cole, whether he realised it at the time or not, significantly widened the parameters for, and dismantled preconceptions of, how Black people and Black players could and should behave.

'I wasn't just playing football for myself, my family, my club, my teammates and the fans,' Cole told me finally. 'I played football for my generation as well. I wanted to try and show my generation that, you can still play football at whatever level it is, but you can actually be yourself. You don't have to jump through any hoops for anybody.'

HOPE POWELL

The Accidental Trailblazer

Jude Wanga

Hope Powell's experience is both an exceptional one and an archetypal one. It is a life that leaps out with the typical frustrations of those who may find their aspirations dismissed and their voices marginalised. Black, a woman, queer, working class. A Black, working-class, queer woman. The term 'intersectional' is an easy one to reach for when writing about a certain experience, or trying to make a certain point, but here it is unavoidable.

But Powell is not simply a collection of protected characteristics. She is a human and often quite a proud one, a self-reliant leader willing to make her own decisions against the backdrop of her own inexperience, despite resistance from individuals and institutions who might obstruct her. Her achievements are remarkable, many of them warranting further examination to appraise her legacy. But just as much can be gleaned from all the times she was let down – not just during her professional career, but in the time leading up to her fifteen-year tenure as coach of the Lionesses.

There are two routes to understanding Powell. There is her early life, during which she was raised on a Peckham council estate with her brother, stepbrothers and stepsister, ricocheting between ingratiating herself with a group of football-mad boys to play in their matches and protecting her mother against the violence meted out by her stepfather. Her ability to negotiate a path through his malevolent presence is perhaps indicative of how she became the groundbreaker we know today but, although she acknowledges that having to shield her mother had 'an effect' on her, she refutes the attribution of her success to his influence.

The other, and perhaps more familiar, route to Powell's story, details her battle with bureaucracy and lack of infrastructural support as a woman attempting to play elite-level football in England. Starting as a player at Millwall Lionesses in 1978 – a team she joined because archaic FA rules banned her from representing her school team past the age of eleven – her aims never changed. 'All I ever wanted was to play the game and fight for the cause of women's football,' she told *Great British Life* in 2020.[1] 'When I started training at 11, there weren't any female professionals. There was no money in the women's game ... we used to train on concrete.'

Powell's battle wasn't solely with institutional elements. She found scant support for her aspirations within her home environment, as she told Carole Cadwalladr in a 2013 *Guardian* profile:

> It was a cultural thing. It just wasn't what West Indian girls were supposed to do. My mother hates it now if she reads that she was against me playing. But she absolutely was. I came home late from training one time, and I had a game on the Sunday, and she was like, that's it: you're not going. But I did. I just sneaked out. Got into trouble. Sneaked out again. I was that *Bend It Like Beckham* girl! I really was. But my mum is my biggest fan now.[2]

Describing Powell simply as a 'manager' does her a gargantuan disservice and minimises the far-reaching consequences of her impact. Yes, she turned England into a serious international side, leading them in six major tournaments – including two

World Cup quarter-finals (2007 and 2011) and a run to the final of the 2009 Euros, where they lost to Germany – but she also spearheaded the drive to make the women's game credible and instilled within it a sense of purpose. Without Powell, the Women's Super League would not exist as it does now, and even the notion of national press coverage for the women's game would be laughable were it not for the progress she oversaw. Her legacy is obvious, wide-ranging, and ineffable.

Writing in her autobiography *Hope: My Life in Football*, Powell revealed she was racially abused once in her playing days, while playing for Friends of Fulham in 1987:

> Oddly, playing for Fulham was the only time in women's football when I was slagged off for being black. In my experience, racism was fairly rare in the women's game back then. That's what made it so surprising. During a game, one of the opposition called me a black something-not-very-nice, which triggered a sequence of events that was like something out of a comedy show. Teammate Brenda [Sempare] completely lost the plot and went for this girl. She started fighting her and soon they went down in a heap on the ground and rolled around on the pitch, belting lumps out of one another.[3]

While a subtle form of racism – particularly in an institutional sense – would reappear and stalk her later in life, her formative experiences of domestic abuse were more prevalent, her recounting of them claustrophobic and inescapable. Perhaps the starkest admission Powell makes is that she considered killing the man who was beating her mother:

> One night I was staying at a friend's place when Mum rang. The frightened tone of her voice terrified me. I knew that

> Carl had been bashing her about again. I asked my friend if I could borrow his car. He tried to stop me, but I went so crazy he relented. I drove over to my mum's house and along the way worked out very specifically what I was going to do. I would quietly let myself in and go straight to the kitchen. I would grab the largest chopping knife and stab him in the chest. If I killed him, so be it. I worked through how I would claim self-defence on behalf of my mum for everything he'd done to her. I hated him. But more than anything, I was worried that if I didn't do for him, he'd do for my mum.[4]

During the years in which the abuse took place, very little care was afforded to victims, who had little recourse to support. Today, more is understood not only about domestic violence but also about the psychological aspect of abuse, and there is a great deal more discussion about how violence against women is both wrong and pervasive. But serious structural reform still feels like a distant target upon which not enough emphasis is placed.

The confession that she was ready to end her stepfather's life shows that Powell was full of self-reliance even then. Although she of course did not follow through with her plan, she did not ask others to resolve a dreadful situation but instead looked within herself to effect change, a quality she drew upon in order to become one of the first and most successful Black female footballers. She would need that ability to look inwards and carry on, given that she had no experience or formal knowledge of how to build an institution.

Before venturing into more troubling terrain, it's important to emphasise that Powell's career was studded with exceptional highs. She gained her first cap for England in 1983 aged sixteen. She earned sixty-six caps in total, and appeared in the 1995

Hope Powell received her first cap for England aged just sixteen. She would go on to represent her country sixty-six times.

World Cup as vice-captain. Powell also played in the 1989 FA Cup Final – a game which she decorated with two well-taken goals – and finished as Millwall Lionesses's record highest scorer. Had her career concluded there, her legend would be set in stone.

But we cannot and should not gloss over how Powell's career also laid bare the struggles of being a footballer in the women's game. Wages were low or non-existent, so Powell had part-time jobs, and held fundraisers for fees and equipment. The costs of rehabilitating a serious injury were covered by her own pocket (the careers of several other women footballers were cut short due to the substandard physical care that was uniform). When it came to setting up the backroom staff for her England side, she had fewer staff members than her equivalent for the men's team had on the subs bench.

The tales she recalls mount up well beyond these examples and reflect the general female experience. Playing as a footballer while also working a second job can be seen as analogous to the modern woman's role as both breadwinner and primary household caregiver. In this way, Powell's successes and achievements are to be doubly admired. The women's game was never meant to be lucrative, and has never been given even half the support the men's game received, but still it grew.

As a child playing football in the nineties, I was coached by members of Arsenal's youth team, which at the time included future England star Rachel Yankey. Over the next few years, my interest in playing dwindled in spite of the steadily increasing popularity of the women's game. It all came too late for me, but who knows what difference the infrastructure Powell was implementing would have made to my decision to give the sport up?

Away from the recurrent difficulties that Powell's journey unavoidably embodies, one thing that leaps out from her experiences is just how much more there remains to do, not only for women, but also for men. After the 2012 London Olympics, the British public were fed the buzzword 'legacy', with billions invested into property redevelopment and poured into companies outsourced to provide substandard services. We witnessed the empty veneration of the NHS at the same time as it was gutted and put under grim strain by those leading the cheers.

This approach to public sporting health was mirrored somewhat in Powell's career at the FA. She had to fight against not just the FA's indifference to women's football but the distaste for giving people something tangible and intangible, communal and personal, that does not stimulate the bottom line. Sport, like art, education and other spiritual activities, is denigrated and undermined if it can't be packaged into some form of exploitable content.

Powell's responsibilities and achievements might not be as pop-culturally significant as Gareth Southgate's – it could be argued that coverage of his waistcoat stretched beyond that afforded to her – but in the long term, the work and influence she wrought are incomparably more significant.

When she took over as England manager, Powell had to fight for access to meetings into which her male peers were brought without question – such as the development of Club England. Not only that, she established youth sides to develop the nation's most talented girls all the way down to under-15s – the kind of programme that takes time and collective effort to establish for men and boys, but which Powell managed in a fraction of the time and with a fraction of the resources.

Speaking to *The Coaches' Voice* in 2017, Powell opened up about her experience of instituting the far-reaching infrastructural change that many now take for granted, and the toll it took on her mental and physical wellbeing:

> Gradually, I started to build it. I'd manoeuvre things, add things, beg for money, do more and more. And it just got bigger and bigger. It meant I was always battling. Every day I went into the FA, it felt like I was in a fight. And I was fighting. I was fighting for women's football. It was tough ... Many people never realised the amount of fighting I had to do. They will never know. It was constant.[5]

Powell established regional centres for her senior players to keep in contact and stay fit while instituting central contracts for the core of her side, helping to convert the top level of the women's game into a professional sport. Finally, the world's best players could make enough money on which to live. And Powell did this without the formal tertiary education that would have assisted her planning, and without any work experience on which to rely. Of course, those are not prerequisites for achieving such transformative effects, but they can make such attempts easier and, rightly or wrongly, engender some level of credibility. To have revolutionised the system nonetheless evidences just what a remarkable woman Powell is.

Powell was not initially keen to be a Black female role model. 'The colour issue? ... I didn't go, "Oh, I'm a black woman,"' she explained to *The Athletic*'s Andy Naylor. However, she knew that once she had made the choice to accept the role as England's first Black football manager, failure was never an option. 'I thought, "Shit, I've got an opportunity, this is what you wanted, you'd better run with it and you cannot fail."' She continued: 'The thing about "I can't fail" was about being a woman and black, so I made every effort to be the best I could be.'[6]

The unfairness of the system means that, while Powell now gets credit for all her firsts, things going wrong might have been used as justification to rule out other Black, queer women getting a similar chance. In fact, looking at the two white men who have succeeded her as manager, one might consider not only that the system was set up to make her success a battle, but that those problems remained entrenched. 'I was female and black,' Powell said to *The Coaches' Voice*. 'The decision-makers? White. Male. And middle-class. That's what it was like. That's what it's still like, I think.'[7]

The problems Powell had to negotiate are as predictable as they are damaging. When taking her 'A' coaching licence, she was repeatedly overlooked when she attempted to answer questions in front of her classmates, never allowed to forget who she was by an FA that continues to go out of its way to express its mistrust in anything but the most limited examples of diversity. In November 2020, Greg Clarke, chairman of the FA, lost his job for crass appraisals of what ethnic minorities and women might want from football. Even after years of campaigning for – at the very least – public acknowledgement of the tenets of political correctness, the basics are still threatened by incompetence and malice.

Powell has written of her belief that she was held back because of who she was and what she represented to those in charge. Studying for her UEFA Pro Licence – the game's highest coaching qualification, of which Powell was the first female recipient – she first had to win over those who should have considered her a peer. Both in the classroom and away from it, groups of men would sit, talk and reminisce as the work was left unfinished, forcing Powell to organise and cajole them so that it got done. But she did not have access to the networks that provided many of them with at least a couple of managerial appointments, and was thereby forced to prove herself not by being their equal but by being their better. It is a familiar refrain among ethnic minorities – and Black people in particular – that, to succeed in the Western world, 'You have to work twice as hard for half as much,' but in a country structured to maintain the hegemony of those with money and connections, Powell is emblematic of a wider injustice.

Though she recognises that plenty of men have been surprisingly helpful – including Howard Wilkinson, who gave her no choice but to attend the aforementioned Pro Licence course, and Alan May, the father figure who coached her at Millwall Lionesses, even creating a tailor-made fitness programme for her – she believes that there were others actively willing

During her thirteen-year tenure as manager of the England women's national football team, Hope Powell fought for revolutionary infrastructural change. Without her influence it's doubtful the Women's Super League would exist as it does today.

her to fail. When she was released by the FA after her team's poor performances at the 2013 Euros, Trevor Brooking, her line manager, was not even present – shoddy behaviour that reflected the unwillingness of the FA and the game as a whole to take her seriously – despite her myriad accomplishments.

During her time as manager, Powell worked so hard that she barely existed as a social being. When she left the FA, Mark Sampson, her replacement, was not the only new appointment. He was given two senior figures who took on some of what had been Powell's responsibilities – or, in other words, she had spent years working too hard and being paid too little, doing the job of three people. This predicament is one with which Black women are painfully familiar.

Throughout her career, Powell emerged as an accidental trailblazer. But, by showing British football that she could be that while staying true to herself and standing against those who would obstruct or ignore her, she offers a template for how Black women can navigate white spaces. Regardless of silence or action, we will often be painted negatively or as inferior in some way, derided as aggressive or bullying. The work done, first by Powell, and then by Anita Asante, Lianne Sanderson, Rachel Yankey and others, has helped to mitigate those insults.

In both a personal and professional context, I have spoken to young Black girls who know no other female managers of Powell's vintage, and see her as a symbol of everything that they could achieve. In a world in which the former England women's manager Mark Sampson had, deliberately or not, made the England national team far from attractive to Black girls by making racist remarks to Eniola Aluko and Drew Spence, Powell demonstrated that it was entirely possible for them to force their way through nonetheless: a young woman from Peckham could sit at the top of the game.

Without Powell, there may have been no Eniola Aluko, whose success in English football took her to Juventus, and who is an outspoken media presence despite the abuse she regularly faces. There would also be no Alex Scott, whose ease in front of the camera has made her a success as a media personality in her own right.

I sometimes wonder if my own experience of playing the game came too early to benefit from the influence of Powell. As I grew up, there was still scepticism that becoming a footballer was a feasible or respectable career for a young woman.

While my school was definitely at the forefront of getting girls into amateur football, to cross that bridge into the professional world was hard without a mentor or guide. I'll never forget being taught how to cross a ball by Rachel Yankey, who was well on her way to becoming a fully fledged player for the England national team. I recognise now that my classmates and I could have progressed even further had we pursued the opportunities presented to us.

I had the chance to have trials with Tottenham and Arsenal's women's sides, but there was little appetite among my friends to attend them. I don't think they had sufficient belief in their ability, or the support from their families to consider football as a potential career option. But now Powell, Scott and Aluko can be held up as examples of what is possible.

Thanks in large part to a new £24 million broadcast deal struck with both Sky Sports and the BBC, the prospect of a long, even lucrative career in the Women's Super League is now open to the best players. While it still might not be a long-term option for some girls who turn pro, the dream of success and glamour is no longer a completely absurd or fantastical endgame. If my friends and I were ten years later to that session with Yankey, then the world would have been more receptive to my dreams, and there would have been greater infrastructure to convert them into palpable sporting progress. But then, had we come along ten years later, would the opportunity to learn from someone like Yankey have existed for us? Time is a funny thing.

Football has been transformed for young girls because of Hope Powell. Where once it was a pastime that raised suspicion from parents or friends, it is now an accepted mainstream hobby, dream and potential career path. The benefits of sport for women continue to be lost on a government which has no interest in funding them but, piece by piece, things are changing as a result of the foundations laid by Powell. 'More and more large companies are wanting to become involved in women's football,' she emphasised in her autobiography. 'It's all a far cry from my early days at Millwall, when we struggled to get local firms to sponsor our boots and shin-pads. I'm proud to have played my part in helping change happen over the past 20 years.'[8]

I see similarities between Powell and me. Her story of having limited experiences with racism as a child reminds me of my own childhood. After being sent from Congo to escape the civil war aged just four, I arrived in North London and quickly became part of a close-knit working-class community, much the same as the one that Powell described in her book:

> On my estate, my friends were like a big extended family. All the gang were sports mad, and if we weren't playing football, we'd be shooting pool and playing table tennis down at the local youth club. That's pretty much all there was to do on the estate. But, on the odd occasion, people did let their hair down together. In 1977, when it was the Queen's Silver Jubilee, we had a really big street party. There were tables out on the road full of food everyone had brought out.[9]

Much like Powell, my friends were of all ethnicities, and while we were more than dimly aware of the presence of racism, it was not something that intruded too harshly on our everyday life.

Powell is now seen as an inspiration and a guide. Women see in her the chance to be great, to achieve something that women have never achieved before. And she did not just succeed: she succeeded as a Black, working-class, queer woman. As she put it in her autobiography:

> I was that little West Indian kid from Juniper Flats council estate in Peckham who had posters of Kevin Keegan and Ray Wilkins on her bedroom wall and played footie with the boys. Now I was sat at my own desk, England manager, working for the oldest FA in the world. Then it dawned on me. This, I realised, is what you call progress. I knew my mum would be proud. That all my loved ones and friends would be made up. But I also realised it was a statement to all people who came from backgrounds like me.[10]

ANITA ASANTE

Saturday Born

Jeanette Kwakye

Ama: by tradition, the Akan name given to a female child born on a Saturday. In Ghanaian folklore, Saturday-borns are fiercely loyal, reliable and generous – characteristics which all ring true in Anita Ama Ankyewah Asante.

Growing up in the diaspora, working-class West Africans born in Britain have lived through a unique set of experiences. Moving between council estates, negotiating traditional gatherings and trying to absorb dialects and cultural practices, while at the same time trying to fit in and assimilate – all while growing up – can be tricky. It adds a thickening layer to an already toughened skin. Especially the skin in which Anita Asante was born.

In an egalitarian world, Anita's identity as a gay British-Ghanaian woman would have no bearing on how she's perceived. But the society we live in ensured that the intersections of her identity have sometimes worked against her. Born in London in 1985 to Ghanaian parents, Anita is a first-born child who bore the burden of many second-generation Black children of the 1980s, regularly reminded that she would have to work 'twice as hard' as her white counterparts just to be seen as equal in society. This mantra, which has inherently pragmatic intentions, also comes with a weight many would prefer not to carry.

Anita was followed by two siblings – Andrew and Annabel, four and ten years younger respectively – and became a big sister in every sense of the word, although her early love for the game didn't inspire either of them to join her. Andrew settled on a career in property management, while Annabel is a make-up sales associate, but both remain ardent supporters of their sister in all that she does.

It's often the case that women footballers are introduced to the game by men, but this wasn't the way things worked with Anita. Her love of football grew independently and was apparent from an early age. 'My mum used to force my brother to come play out with me, so I'd drag him along, and put him in goal,' she told me. 'He still hates me for it.'

The football cage on the Edgware-based Stonegrove estate that Anita called home was the only patch of green around the back of the flats, an environment in which local kids would express themselves until it grew too dark to continue their small-sided matches. They called the cage 'Wembley'. It was just six miles away from the real Wembley, where Anita would eventually realise so many dreams.

Anita describes the cage as the place where she had to play to gain the respect of her male peers. To get in the cage in the first place, you had to be good. To then thrive in a space defined by hyper-masculine energy, you had to be full of confidence and belief. It was a big deal to be allowed to play in there as a girl, even for a self-confessed tomboy. But it's an even bigger deal – the scrutiny grows more intense – when you're one of the best, even at the tender age of eight.

Just ask Allan Bland, a childhood neighbour of Anita's. He would give a regular knock for her to come out and 'kick ball' when her little brother had had enough of playing tag along. He was white, male and working class, but at that age it didn't matter, their council-estate bubble meaning they found a commonality through their shared experiences. He introduced Anita to more of the boys on the estate, and this co-sign would mark him as one of the first of many allies in her life. Of course, over time her allies would start to look and act markedly differently.

Confusingly for Anita, Allan's respect was confined to the estate. At school, kicking her ball onto the roof and a constant stream of teasing were his ways of getting her attention. But at least she knew she had his acceptance where it mattered: in the cage. Was this a sign of things to come perhaps? Respect on the field of play, but not so much elsewhere?

Anita describes a football as 'the easiest toy you can get' and recalls memories of her great uncle George Adjei, who would come down from Birmingham in the summer and watch games with her. 'The first thing I wanted to do when I came back from school was play football,' she said. 'I always had a ball at my feet.'

Her family realised almost immediately that her talent and desire were special: 'I never had to tell my parents that I wanted to play, they just knew.' Like many West African mothers, Ernestina Asante made every effort to ensure that her daughter excelled at everything she tried. But cultural norms dictated that her main priority was making sure her daughter excelled academically. This meant that the local comprehensive would not suffice. Anita's journey to school became that little bit longer, taking her across town to Mill Hill County High School, in order to satisfy the standards set by her mother. However, Anita made sure that both her schoolwork and football received the same amount of attention.

The secondary school ecosystem can be brutal. Set in the context of puberty, life can be varied and definitive. Anita understood the power of football and how that would help her to navigate the playground landscape. At Mill Hill, she quickly realised that gaining the respect of the boys was equally important at school as it was on the estate. However, her proximity to the boys also meant she became the reluctant go-between for the girls with more romantic interests. 'I thought I was really low-key, but I guess people really knew me as "Neetz the footballer",' she told me. 'I was more of an introvert in an interpersonal way. My way to be bold was to do the things I enjoyed. Playing football in my skirt and shoes that would get bruk up from playing with the boys.' This continues to be Anita's modus operandi – she is not afraid of judgement.

For many professional women footballers, the experience of having to make do with the boys' teams until it became physically impossible to play – or when the boys, and their parents, started to complain – is widely shared. Anita was fortunate that, in the later stages of her attendance, her school formed a girls' team. While far more commonplace today, at the time girls' school teams were almost unheard of, and helped to shape a different mindset that bit earlier for the players involved and their parents. If your teachers think that playing football is something you can do, then the question moves from 'Why?' to 'Why not?' This was one of the many subtle, localised changes that positively impacted the landscape of the women's game today.

One of the first formative moments in Anita's life came in the form of a fax sent to her school. Arsenal women were holding local trials for girls and Ms Harding, her enthusiastic PE teacher, suggested that she make the trip to Burnt Oak:

> I dragged some schoolmates with me. To be honest we were very casual about it – we didn't even believe it was the real Arsenal, we thought it was a fake Arsenal. A big part of the ignorance of not knowing much about the women's game or knowing it existed at all really.

In the early nineties, moments like this were pivotal. It wasn't often you'd hear that a West African household had thrown support behind their children when it came to sport – especially girls, for whom pathways to professionalism seemed so scarce. But Anita's parents bucked the trend. It helped that her father, Kwame, was a massive Arsenal fan. 'He would've dropped everything, done anything, to get me there,' she said.

The closeness of Anita's relationship with her parents allowed her to flourish and have confidence in her ability. This meant she was able to go into that first trial free of undue pressure and just play. She wanted to show the coaches what she was about. Anita continued to impress, and was offered a place at the club's centre of excellence in 1999.

The history of women's football in England is ugly, a truth from which many in the upper echelons of the FA shy away. The complexity of the game and its relationship with women in England is heavy to say the least. Anita's entry point into football came just twenty-five years after the FA's ban on women's football was lifted. The brutal decision, made on 5 December 1921, was born of bigotry and fear. Dick, Kerr Ladies* were at the height of their fame and drawing crowds of 53,000 to Goodison Park, which led those in charge to fear the usurpation of the men's game.

Such a devastating power-play would change the course and culture of women's football, setting it back decades. When

* Dick, Kerr Ladies FC was one of the earliest known women's association football teams in England. The team remained in existence for over forty-eight years, from 1917 to 1965. During its early years, matches attracted anywhere from 4,000 to over 50,000 spectators. In 1920, Dick, Kerr Ladies defeated a French side 2–0 in front of 25,000 people, a match that went down in history as the first international women's association football game. The team faced strong opposition from the Football Association, who banned the women from using fields and stadiums controlled by affiliated clubs for fifty years.

it eventually returned, women were not playing for the dizzying heights of fame or financial reward found in the men's game, and even now the imbalance persists. Underfunded teams, poor or non-existent facilities, the inevitability of online abuse and a lack of proper medical care mean that women footballers must possess innate drive and determination to make it as a professional player and withstand the difficulties such a career entails.

Anita has all the necessary characteristics but her journey to the top was not always intentional, her path not deliberately carved out. 'Not until I was in a structured set-up at Arsenal, did I learn more about the game,' she said. 'I was thinking, "When I am done with school, I am going to be a psychologist."' It took a lot of exposure and convincing for her to realise that professional football was something that she could make a career of.

Asante stands on the shoulders of giants: Mary Phillip, Arsenal teammate, England women's first senior Black captain and now manager of non-league Peckham Town FC; Hope Powell, a pioneer on the pitch who would later manage Anita in two World Cups and the 2012 Olympics. Then there was Rachel Yankey, the dazzling forward who could light up the left wing but took on many roles. 'From that early moment of connecting with Rachel', Anita recalled, 'I just wanted to know more, I wanted to know how far I could get in the game. She was super-friendly, open, chatty, supportive. She made me feel as if she was always putting a big arm around me.'

Another black woman of Ghanaian heritage, confident in her ability and from North West London: the alignment was too strong to ignore. The power generated by Rachel's visibility is what Anita needed to realise that football was about to become life. The bar was set. For Anita, Rachel represented another ally – one who got it, who understood her and saw the potential and ability from the off. They would go on to be team-mates for club and country, and the two remain close friends.

The environment at Arsenal challenged Anita to push on and aim for sporting greatness, but one day a week of training was not enough (the mantra of having to work 'twice as hard' was loud and ever-present). So, it was back to the cage to

Anita Asante joined Arsenal's centre of excellence in 1998. During the 2006–07 season, she won the quadruple – UEFA Cup, League, League Cup and FA Cup, before departing for cross-town rivals Chelsea in 2008.

subsidise the lack of practice with a grit and determination that cannot be taught. Anita developed into a quietly confident, technical player who was both composed and assured on the ball while also a brilliant reader of the game, solid in her decision-making as a defender.

Alongside fellow Black players Lianne Sanderson, Mary Phillip, Alex Scott and Rachel Yankey, Anita became part of an Arsenal side who, under Vic Akers, were the pioneers of the women's game in the early 2000s. Their side was so strong and their dominance so pronounced that in the 2006–07 season they did the unthinkable: they won four major trophies, showing the world what can be done with the right level of investment and strategy.

At the time, the popularity of the men's team was at its peak, making legends out of Thierry Henry, Freddie Ljungberg and Robin van Persie, and with talents rich and diverse enough to be a great marketing tool for the women's team in a 'one-club' culture. But, much to Anita's annoyance, the women's performances did not receive the adoration and respect they warranted; instead they were treated as an afterthought. To her, this was a sign that things still had a long way to go:

> There is always a consciousness in the women's game; you'd hear senior players tell you what it used to be like. You are very aware of what the differences are and what the barriers are. You only had to look around at a big club like Arsenal and see the men's set-up and the academies, and know, you know, that you're nowhere near getting that, or having that foundation and resource.

Despite the unfairness of this situation, Anita radiated calm when discussing it – but this should not be mistaken for apathy. Her ability to plan and observe are key, both to her play on the pitch and strategy away from it. Even after winning every club honour, she was desperate for more, all the more so after England were beaten by the USA in the quarter-finals of the 2007 World Cup. She forced herself to break away from the club that had nurtured and believed in her ability from the start, a tough but necessary decision. As grateful as she was for everything and everyone that Arsenal had given her, Anita realised she had to prioritise her ambition.

During the summer of 2008, she moved across London to Chelsea, along with Lianne Sanderson. This was a shock move, especially given the dominance of the club she was leaving, but she wanted to be part of something special at Stamford Bridge, by helping to develop a side able to compete against her former one – much to the annoyance of her former boss. But after just a season at Chelsea, the lure of the shiny new Women's Professional Soccer league in the USA became too much, the opportunity too enticing to ignore. So, Anita moved to New Jersey to play in a competition that had no historical pedigree but significant financial backing.

The USA has long been seen as the Mecca for women's football, but Anita's arrival was to be both a baptism into professional sport and an introduction to the American gaze. With players traded at pace like commodities, the energy of the league was unlike anything Anita had ever experienced. Other English players also made the move stateside roughly around the same time, including Lianne Sanderson, Eniola Aluko, Alex Scott and Kelly Smith, each of whom have their own tales of the experience.

For Anita, who had enjoyed the stability of staying at Arsenal for so many years, four clubs in three seasons – from 2009 to 2011, Anita would turn out for Sky Blue FC, Saint

Louis Athletica, Chicago Red Stars, Washington Freedom and Sky Blue FC again – was not what she was expecting. But the traits of tenacity, grit and determination that she had picked up in the cage would prove invaluable as she switched from state to state, and ultimately she was fortified by this unique challenge she could not have experienced anywhere else: 'Footballing wise, it brought out the competitiveness in me. It taught me to be more aggressive. That culture in general, it brings out your personality. They expressed themselves a lot more.'

But this experience came at a cost: often, Anita felt isolated. It was the first time she had left the comfort of home, and relationships she formed were quickly crushed as she moved from state to state. Her time in St Louis was a particular low point, leaving her feeling 'shifted and shafted', as decisions about her career were made without her involvement. The volatility of the Women's Professional Soccer league saw it fold within five years and Anita's time in the States came to an end. She had to move quickly. Most expected a return to England, especially given the imminent London Olympics, but it was the Damallsvenskan* that came calling.

Sweden was never really on Asante's radar until Therese Sjögran, a teammate at the New Jersey team Sky Blue FC, mentioned it. The lure of the Women's Super League wasn't quite strong enough to draw Anita home. Instead she headed to Göteborg FC, where she found an atmosphere that matched the energy she was searching for at that point in her career: 'The first two years [in Sweden] were so fun and positive. After all the highs and lows of the American experience, I needed a place that was stable and relaxed, a warm and open environment.'

* The Damallsvenskan, also known as OBOS Damallsvenskan for sponsorship reasons, is the highest division of women's football in Sweden.

That environment allowed her to thrive personally, which in turn allowed her to express a different side of her game. Her form at Göteborg would lead to her selection for the 2012 Olympics, and, though Great Britain had never previously sent a team to the Games, fractious relationships between the FA's home countries were put aside and Anita was able to take centre stage and make history.

The FA's ability to perpetually disappoint women is self-evident, and there was no women's team at the 2016 Olympics. But the most recent egregious example is the case that engulfed Eniola Aluko who, in 2016, reported England coach Mark Sampson for race-related bullying and harassment. A highly public battle, which involved character assassinations, hot takes and opinion pieces, endured for months. It was clear there was serious disharmony in the set-up and not everyone was on Team Eni. In fact, public displays of support for Sampson from current teammates added fuel to the fire.

Anita had been a mainstay of the England team, but was dropped by Sampson ahead of the 2015 World Cup. She had her own issues with the way he treated her, which she has chosen not to divulge. But Anita, along with Lianne Sanderson, stood by Eni, defending her vociferously and urging people to believe her side of the story. She was determined to offer support to a fellow Black player whatever the cost. 'To see how isolated she was in this shocked me,' Asante said:

> A lot of people took objective views, based on the views that we have known as Black women in this country for decades, we are at the bottom of the totem pole. And if you have an issue or if you bring up something, then you're just angry. It gets projected backwards. Then it becomes character assassination. I wasn't having that.

Women's football in the UK was flying high at the time, with recognisable faces, fresh approaches and a Women's Super League being pumped with investment. This raised the stakes for a number of individuals, though we can only speculate about whether this explains why so many failed to speak out. For the Black women in the set-up, in the darkest moments, the silence from many of the non-white members of the Lionesses squad was deafening. 'Everyone is looking individually at what do I have to gain or lose? It just doesn't directly affect them, so why are they gonna put their neck out?' said Asante. 'They have endorsements and contracts as national players. For a lot of players, that's high-stakes stuff.' All of a sudden, the passion and integrity that the women were known for was being compromised.

The impact of all this left a huge imprint on Anita. How many young Black women watched that episode unfold, saw how little support Aluko was offered by both media and teammates, and thought, *I'd love to be part of that one day*? 'The outcome is not positive for young Black girls,' Asante said:

> It left so many questions: 'Is it really like that at the top? Do I want that? Am I going to have to filter myself and do the mental gymnastics?' These are the questions that are being asked by young talent at a grassroots level. None of these questions or scenarios are about performance, on how to be one of the best players. In fact, all the above amplifies everything that is wrong with the women's game at the elite level for women of colour.

This impression is reflected in reality. In the past ten years, only fourteen Black players have been capped by England – that's nineteen per cent of the total, relative to forty-nine per cent in the men's game during the same period. These numbers are not any better in age-group football, which suggests that we're stuck with the status quo for a while yet. A quick scan of Women's Super League squads shows a similarly stark picture.

Had the Aluko v Sampson episode happened in the USA, things might have unfolded differently. Culturally, women athletes have greater freedom to speak up and unionise there. 'The difference [from] the USA team,' Anita explained, 'is that we [in the UK] are not very good as a collective. To even have a discussion as a team, everything was still led by management and staff. There is no individual advocacy and empowerment.'

Anita watched on from Sweden, willing more players and staff to publicly display their support for Aluko. But they did not. So she looked towards Black men for allyship, and they too fell short. Not one male footballer spoke out against Aluko's treatment. 'If I see discrimination against a Black boy or Black man,' Asante said, 'especially in sport, I am the first one to bat for them or support their cause. But it's the same feeling again: why do Black women have to beg for support from Black men within our own community?'

Anita empathises with the plight of Black men in football as she does with that of Black people across the globe. She understands why the Black Lives Matter movement in 2020 penetrated the minds of the masses. The murder of George Floyd explicitly played out to millions of people, struck chords and touched nerves. In the summer of 2020, it was en vogue to show solidarity with Black people. For some, that meant reading anti-racism literature; others posted a black square on social media. For the English footballing world, it meant taking a knee before games.

For some, taking a knee is a contentious act of protest, but critics, including Crystal Palace's Wilfried Zaha, view it now as an empty gesture. In the main, it's still understood as absolutely necessary. For Anita, the impact of the act must not be watered down: 'We are Black people every single day, and that is not going to change.'

A few other high-profile Black voices in the game are sceptical. Les Ferdinand has argued that taking a knee has been 'diluted', a view that didn't surprise Anita. She sees how anti-racism campaigns can appear cynical, how the sentiment can feel disingenuous. But she counters this by insisting that public displays, policy making and strategic action should be working together in tandem: 'For the people behind the scenes that might not like the fact that the game is being "hijacked" by player activism … As a player, I'm thinking the quickest way you're gonna get me to stop kneeling is to do something.' And, as a member of FIFPRO's (Fédération Internationale des Associations de Footballeurs Professionnels) Global Player Council – a group working to transfer intelligence from pitch to boardroom – Anita is striving to make that happen.

The twilight years of any professional athlete's career can be tricky, with the prospect of retirement on the horizon. For many, the idea of doing something other than the only thing they've known causes confusion and panic: the lack of planning, direction and self-confidence can precipitate a huge identity crisis. For those with the foresight to plan, the transition can be relatively painless. But to start again in different space requires support, allies and sometimes a big dose of humility.

Admitting that she has, at most, two seasons left at Aston Villa – the club she was brought to in 2020 by Aluko, its technical director, after two seasons back at Chelsea – Anita is on the case. Throughout her career, she has built a solid platform enabling her to be seen as a prominent voice in football. High on her agenda at FIFPRO is helping people understand what it means to be a gay footballer. Having coming out aged twenty-three,

Anita has had time to grow comfortable in her own skin, and although her journey has been difficult at times, women's football is mostly a safe space for players to express their sexuality.

'The nature of women in general is to be slightly more open and understanding,' said Asante. 'It's the nurturing element of the women's game that has allowed people to be more open about who they are.' Conversations around sexuality in the game have become significantly more progressive in recent years. Organisations like Stonewall campaign with creativity and enthusiasm and, as a result, it is becoming more and more unacceptable to publicly voice archaic views about the LGBTQ community.

Yet the elephant still remains in the room: not one current player in the English men's league has come out. There are various reasons for this: PR specialists have warned against it, or lingering fears about acceptance, whether from teammates or crowds. Even though numerous charities are able to offer support, this fear is still deeply rooted. Having spoken up on football's historical problems with the LGBTQ community, it has become clear to Anita that the remedy is to change the language, both casual and deliberate, found across media and in wider football culture that works to exclude.

If people are prevented from expressing themselves honestly, they are more likely to struggle with life, and in football that is likely to manifest on the pitch. 'I hope the younger generation now feel more empowered,' Anita said, 'because as a younger person, I didn't have that ... that confidence and self-esteem to be my authentic self.'

Few footballers and few people stand for as much as Anita, and her relentless positivity has much to do with her success. Considering the cards life dealt her and the world in which we live, things could easily have been very different. Like all of us, she will continue to dream and believe, football the backdrop to her life.

'I feel like if I owned a club, I could ensure all the opportunities are there, for girls in particular, from all backgrounds. That would be amazing.'

No one who knows Anita would put it past her.

DANNY ROSE

The Anti-footballer

Kwaku Dapaah-Danquah

When I began writing this essay, Danny Rose was still contracted to Tottenham Hotspur. However, he'd been completely ostracised from the first team (his last game for Tottenham took place on Saturday 11 January 2020). A six-month loan to fellow Premier League side Newcastle United in the January transfer window didn't turn into a permanent transfer; instead, Rose returned to his parent club that summer and had been turning out for Tottenham's under-23 side – the modern day equivalent of being sent to play with the reserves. Although Rose has now signed for Watford, the manner of his departure was an inglorious end to a career at Spurs that saw him become a fixture for both club and country. Only three years ago he was appearing in the 2019 Champions League Final against Liverpool, and he was still representing England during the Euro 2020 qualifiers. The reasons for his banishment to his club's development squad are shrouded in mystery. While *All or Nothing*,[1] the Amazon documentary series about Tottenham's 2019 season, sought to cast Rose as a combustible character – a clipped-up scene in which Rose and the club's notoriously prickly manager, José Mourinho, clash over Rose's lack of playing time went viral – he is, according to those closest to him, a calm and measured individual more in touch with reality than average football fans may be prepared to believe.

From opening up about his personal struggles with mental health, to his criticism of the football authorities' response to anti-Black racism and the COVID-19 pandemic, his statements have voiced the concerns of many – particularly those disproportionately affected by the ill effects of both pandemics – while simultaneously placing him at odds with establishment figures. In the past, players' reluctance to publicly express views on such 'taboo' subjects perpetuated a sanitised narrative in football – one which was apolitical and arguably void of social awareness altogether – but today, albeit slowly, this appears to be changing. We have pertinent examples of Black players like Raheem Sterling taking to Instagram to urge young Brits to register to vote in the UK 2019 General Election, or Marcus Rashford's incredible feat of pressuring the Conservative government to repeal their decision to scrap free school meals in 2020 through an open letter posted on Twitter.* The fact that players, especially Black ones, are beginning to use their platforms to political effect is a drastic shift from times gone by, and they have been – rightfully – commended for it.

Nonetheless, for me, a Black man with a peripheral interest in football, Danny Rose is a breath of fresh air, distinguished from his peers by virtue of his almost disarming sense of pessimism. He doesn't strike the tone of an activist with an authoritative call-to-action. He simply says what he – and, I'd argue, what the average Black man or woman gisting at the barber's or salon – thinks: when it comes to racism in football, he doesn't believe anything can or will change. It is far from positive, but no less valid.

Rose's pessimism is a warning for wider society. If a millionaire footballer is not insulated from racial abuse, harassment and microaggressions, nor impervious to their psychological effects, how are 'normal' Black people faring?

* On 16 June 2020, the Conservative government agreed to provide free schools meals over the summer (they had initially refused to do so, despite the national lockdown caused by the COVID-19 pandemic). Rashford, whose open letter was posted the day before, was credited with playing a key part in forcing the government to U-turn on their decision.

Rose's candidness has made him one of the most compelling and relatable Black footballers of his generation.

Toxic Privilege

One of the beautiful things about being a child is the lack of limits; every possibility projects endlessly into the future, with every dream seemingly attainable.

I have a hazy memory of sitting in a primary school classroom and a teacher asking us all what we wanted to be when we were older. I can't remember what I said – I think even back then I was subject to chronic generalism. But I do recall that, as each kid put their hand up to share, every boy – bar maybe two or three – said that they wanted to be a footballer. Asking that same question today in any adventure playground, or in any council estate's football cage in the country, would elicit the same response I suspect.

Football occupies many roles. For fans, it can be the lifeblood of friendships and the common bond between strangers. It is often the source of fond memories, the topic of the WhatsApp group and a staple fixture in a weekly calendar. Football is an institution. Football is a religion. This analogy may sound extreme, but it isn't all that far-fetched. There are governing bodies, denominations, acts of worship, days of observance – there are even hymns. But, as with any religion, the purity of its core is easily corrupted by its leaders and devotees alike. As a result, capitalistic exploitation, toxic masculinity and white supremacy have sullied the game since its inception.

The systemic issues deeply rooted in football do not exist within a vacuum; rather, they are a symptom of wider societal failures. But the decision to turn a blind eye to how these issues manifest in the world of football is pervasive. The historical apathy of the establishment about racism or players' mental health, for example, isn't hard to explain. Acknowledging these problems in any meaningful way would require radical steps to be taken to combat them, but football is a massively profit-driven sector. Unless economic interests necessitate such an intervention, there is no real incentive for it. A valuable question to ask is, what are the repercussions for *not* tackling these issues?

At the time of writing, European football is booming. In the 2018–19 season, market revenue hit a record €28.9 billion – a continuation of the year-on-year growth experienced before the COVID-19 pandemic instituted national lockdowns across the globe.* With the game's chief metric of success at an all-time high, expecting issues of morality to be prioritised over profit would be unrealistic.

Despite the self-evident lack of progress made, for instance, in eradicating racial abuse from the game, the industry continues to demonstrate an indifference that has privileged authorities with a complacency that stifles any real impetus for transformation. Inevitably, it is the Black players that suffer.

> *It's not surprising. This is now normal for black players to receive this kind of abuse after a football match!!! A f*cking game!!!*
>
> *When will these platforms do more. They literally do not care! The racist abuse never ends. Long after the final whistle it is there for everyone to see.*
>
> *Don't tell me about trolls or bots or whose fans it is! It's real people behind these comments.*
>
> – Ian Wright, Instagram, 28 January 2021

Mental Fitness

> *You don't know how long you've got left in football and you're as good as anything one day and you're expendable the next. Literally, nobody is safe. Everybody has a price in football, and sometimes when you get to a certain age,*

* The latest statistics publicly available on Statista are for the 2018–19 season. It can be anticipated that this growth trend will see a dip due to the pandemic.

or you have certain amount of years left on your contract, people who work within a football club will think now it's time to move somebody on and get someone younger in. And it's a business that aims to make money, so yeah, you have to try not to take that too personally.

– Danny Rose, *All or Nothing: Tottenham Hotspur*

It's easy to paint a picture of the soulless corporate machine disregarding the wellbeing of its players, but it would be misleading to deny the complicity of its fans. With all the conditioned allure of the game, footballers unquestionably hold an enviable position in society. They live their childhood dream and enjoy the exuberant trappings that come with it, including extreme wealth and the adoration of millions. Through the rose-tinted glasses of celebrity, the modern footballer is the star of a fantastical drama that has long captivated the world stage, but under the callous lens of capitalism, he is a tradable commodity. It is this interplay between the almost-deified hero and the fallible, dispensable mortal that exposes the ugly realities of life for many players of the beautiful game, who are long overdue a sympathetic ear.

Every element of professional football is subject to intense pressure. The pursuit of a career as a player – which is wrought with undue stresses from a frighteningly young age – highlights the early priming towards mental health declines, particularly in view of the fact that players have a 0.012 per cent chance of graduating through the academy ranks to a Premier League squad, which Michael Calvin has described as 'the sort of chances of you being hit by a meteorite on your way home'.[2] Sadly, an example of how this oft-ignored dark side to the game can materialise is the tragic death of eighteen-year-old Jeremy Wisten, a former Manchester City academy player who took his own life in October 2020 following his release from the club after an injury the previous year.*

> *When it feels like there is no meaning for you to be part of the team, or – I'll go to the extreme – of life also, then that's when it becomes a problem. Because it's like 'Why am I here? What am I doing? What's the goal?'*
>
> – Thierry Henry, 2019[3]

Yet, even for success stories like Danny Rose, who is a product of the Leeds United youth academy, incessant pressures of other forms are inherent in football and uniquely pronounced for Black players. Unlike traditional industries, where work is done behind closed doors, football is a spectacle for public consumption. Fans punctuate the mundanities of everyday life with the victories and defeats of their clubs of choice, projecting their own successes or failures onto these weekly fixtures.

At the highest level of the game, a player is susceptible to negativity on an unprecedented scale – crowds of booing fans, barrages of hateful comments from faceless entities on social media. Of course, the opposite is also true: performing well may result in an entire stadium chanting songs of praise, or a hefty financial bonus. Both the peaks and troughs can be intoxicating – indeed, the rapid oscillation between extreme highs and desolate lows is perhaps the most toxic aspect.

The psychological impact of this fickle glorification and vilification, together with grief and trauma players endure while expected to perform at a high level, are not often spoken

* Although it is outside the scope of this essay, there is a conversation that needs to be had about systems to support young players whose professional ambitions are cut short.

Danny Rose in action for England against the Czech Republic during a UEFA Euro 2020 qualifying match.

about. As is the case for celebrities in general, footballers exude an otherworldliness that has a tendency to dehumanise them. For Black players, the racial tinge of this dehumanisation is innate, and adds extra layers to the problem.*

Danny Rose has arguably faced every manner of trauma imaginable on and off the pitch, stretching back as far as his

* To illustrate this point with a recent example: Following Manchester United's 2–1 loss to Sheffield United on 26 January 2021, the Instagram accounts of 23-year-old Axel Tuanzebe (who was born in DR Congo) and 25-year-old Anthony Martial (of Guadeloupean descent) were littered with comments from troll accounts calling them 'slaves', 'monkeys', 'black cunts' and 'niggers'. Mélanie Martial Da Cruz, Martial's wife, revealed an even more sinister side to the online abuse, including death threats directed at the couple and their two-year-old son.

early years as an academy player at Leeds United. On various occasions he has recounted how he and now-Everton midfielder and friend Fabian Delph were called 'black cunts' at age fourteen. He remembers being surrounded by Serbian players and slapped twice in the aftermath of the England under-21s' victory against Serbia in 2012. He has admitted that the memories of this abuse were at the forefront of his mind when he and other players were subject to monkey chants and missiles in the Euro 2020 qualifier in Montenegro.

Rose's openness about his experiences is bold and unapologetic, but it is his courage to share how they have impacted him psychologically that makes him so compelling for me. The significance of these events and others in the deterioration of his mental health was detailed soberly in what became a landmark interview with Miguel Delaney, chief football writer at *The Independent*.[4]

Despite the long list of ordeals, Rose attributed his mental decline to a series of triggering events condensed over a period of less than a year. In 2017, he sustained an injury to his left knee which rendered him incapable of playing for eight months – abruptly cutting short an encouraging spell of high performance for his team – with his injury arguably prolonged by poor medical advice from staff. Rose told Delaney about how his mood took a turn for the worse, experiencing bouts of anger and reclusiveness during his attempts at regaining fitness as he desperately sought medical interventions to no avail:

> I had cortisone/PRP [platelet rich plasma] injections trying to be fit for my club, and I had to have an op four months down the line – after all that football I missed, when the team was flying and I was playing well, I was playing really

> well, the team were playing really well. Seeing the lads beat Arsenal comfortably, seeing them beat Man United comfortably – it was hard. I'm not saying I've had worse treatment than anyone else. That's football. But it was difficult. That was the start of it.

This alone is more than enough to cause any player to spiral into a depressive state. However, he also revealed that a relentless succession of other events also unfolded at the same time, causing a despair that foreshadowed a diagnosis of clinical depression:

> Nobody knows this, either, but my uncle hung himself in the middle of my rehab, and that triggered it [depression] as well. It was really hard, and being referred to a doctor and psychologist [by the Spurs doctor] helped me massively to cope ... But off the field, there have been other incidents – in August, my mum was racially abused back home in Doncaster. She was very angry and upset about it, and then someone came to the house and nearly shot my brother in the face. Stuff like that was happening throughout my rehab and it was a testing time. A gun was fired at my house, yeah.

No Support

In the normal world, such traumatic experiences would naturally be followed by periods of grief. But grief is an emotion that is seldom afforded to football players. In his 2019 essay for *The Athletic*, Adam Crafton explores the relationship between grief and football in conversation with five former players and managers.[5] The personal tragedies that each of them endured while desperately attempting to stem a bleed into their performances makes for bleak reading. In line with my experience of how men of a certain disposition typically deal with mental anguish, the common thread that the interviewees all shared was a fear of appearing weak to their teammates and losing favour with their clubs – again highlighting the hostile environment to men's vulnerability that is prevalent in football. I have no doubt that this reality is what influences many to speak out only after they have retired from the game. Danny Rose is quite exceptional in this respect. Although he has said that interventions from the Spurs doctor massively helped him to cope, he has since admitted that his candidness about his struggles had some negative reverberations. A coach from an unnamed club that was exploring the possibility of signing him from Tottenham at the time asked to meet in person, 'just to check that [he wasn't] crazy'.[6]

This coach's dismissiveness of Rose's experience is representative of a wider lack of concern for the psychological capacities of Black players, a disregard for the fact that they – like all people – go through things that profoundly affect their wellbeing. If white players, as demonstrated in Crafton's essay, struggle to process and communicate their trauma after universally understood events like the loss of loved ones, what more can be expected from Black footballers, who have the added burden of dealing with injustices of which large swathes of the British population are either insensitive or wilfully ignorant?

This is intimately linked to their dehumanisation as Black people, but accentuated by their positions of wealth. A popular-but-misguided notion that some fans are guilty of perpetuating is that, because Black players are paid so much, they should be impervious to abuse and accept the pernicious elements of their jobs as part of the territory.* Yes, footballers get paid a lot of money. However, the claim that players are grossly overpaid is inherently foolish and easily exploded. Players earn as much as they do because the industry that they work in, as previously discussed, generates billions in revenue. Their salaries are in line with the amount of money generated by the integral role they play in the great spectacle that is modern football. The argument that Black players should be impervious to mental health or willing to silently suffer because of how much they are remunerated is absurd.

Similar sentiments were projected at Stormzy following a response he gave to the question of whether Britain is still racist in an interview with Italian newspaper, *la Repubblica.* Stormzy had the gall to answer in the affirmative. Ironically, the backlash he received from sections of the right-wing media contingent, demanding that he be grateful to the country for 'allowing' him to become successful ultimately proved his point.[8] Rose is fully cognisant that many people view him in a similar light. As he said on Second Captains podcast *The Player's Chair*, 'Whenever I do say things or complain about things, you hear people say "You're on this money so get on with it" ... I just give up with hoping things will change because that's some people's mentality towards racism.'[9]

> *For black people, the impact of trauma passed on from generation to generation through the slave trade, through the years of colonialism and through the hidden micro-aggressions of a proclaimed post-racist society is hugely significant in shaping the mind as well as shaping mental health. Black*

* Studies have shown evidence of the 'dehumanisation thesis', whereby many people subconsciously associate Black people with apes. Paul Butler provides an interesting exploration of this in a 2019 *Guardian* article.[7]

> *men keenly feel the humiliation embedded in these generationally transmitted experiences. Through the forces of a black male identity, black men often develop toward relationships without intimacy and prioritising being strong over acknowledging vulnerabilities.*
>
> – Eugene Ellis, director of the Black, African and Asian Therapy Network[10]

Pessimism

In a climate in which football's governing bodies continue to fail to ensure the safety of Black players from racial abuse and fail to appropriately sanction the perpetrators, there is little reason for any of us to be optimistic about the future. As Rose said in a 2019 interview,[11] 'When countries get fined what I probably spend on a night out in London what do you expect? ... So that's where we're at now in football. Until there's a harsh punishment, there's not much else we can expect.'

His pessimism might be unconventional by football's standards, but it is not unique. He bears the same exhaustion that the Black diaspora have borne for years. We are regularly reminded that expecting change to come from within a society where white supremacy is deeply entrenched is a pursuit for fool's gold. Inequality in systems of education, employment, policing and housing – the pillars of society – reflect this reality. Discussing how white supremacy manifests in football is a useful exercise for highlighting how marginalisation entangles even the most extraordinarily privileged segments of the community, but ultimately it is just a microcosm of a bigger game that is being played – a game in which Black people are often the losers.

There are only so many protests, Twitter threads and diversity and inclusion workshops that one can engage with before disillusionment creeps in. There are only so many recommendations and flaccid displays of 'solidarity' – black-and-white armbands, 'Kick It Out' posters, black-out social media posts, Black Lives Matter T-shirts, one-minute silences and kneels – that we can be sold as signs of progress. 2020's string of highly publicised anti-Black violence, including the murder of George Floyd by the Minneapolis police, the murder of Ahmaud Arbery by white gunmen in Georgia and the death of Belly Mujinga following a racist assault in London have brought this to the fore.

When all of this is put in context of the centuries of racist oppression through slavery, colonialism, police harassment, deaths in police custody, police negligence and everything else, I feel like an increasing number of Black people are one viral video, one racist slur, or one microaggression away from complete disengagement. Rose's voice can thus be viewed as an addition to the growing chorus of Black people in the UK and abroad that are vocally or otherwise communicating: 'Fuck it, I'm done.' This is an attitude that is much less palatable than that of, say, Raheem Sterling, who, although critical of the establishment's response to racism, has used his influence to help to reform the system while discouraging Black players from walking off the pitch in the event of abuse. Rose, on the other hand, has publicly stated that he would do just that if confronted again by on-pitch abuse, and, what's more, has claimed that he is actually looking forward to finishing his football career.*

'How I programme myself is that I think I've got five or six more years left in football, and I just can't wait to see the back

* In an Instagram live interview with @don.emusic, and perhaps in a manner more akin to a conversation between friends, Rose has even suggested that in certain circumstances, if he were to hear racist abuse in a game, he would try to 'write someone off'. Again, not what you might expect to hear from a professional player, but not unlike what many Black men have expressed before.

of it,' Rose said in an interview with *Mirror Sport*.[12] In a subsequent interview with Sky Sports he elaborated on this position:

> People ask me if I want to do my coaching badges. Why? You [retired Black players] are not given a chance, so no, I wouldn't be looking forward to doing my badges – it is a waste of time. That is what I meant [when I said] I am looking forward to calling it day when the time is right.[13]

To many people, these statements were an insult to the game. There is a persistent idea that Black players have a responsibility to push down their frustrations, use their suffering for some esoteric greater good and combat racism by continuing to show up, by not letting the racists 'win'. I respect the perspective of Sterling and others who take this approach – whatever works to keep players sane in the face of adversity is valid. However, I am disappointed when the 'Keep calm and carry on' rhetoric is lauded as the only commendable way of dealing with abuse.

In a BBC Radio 5 Live interview, former Tottenham Hotspur and England midfielder Jermaine Jenas claimed that Danny Rose should simply overcome his resentment towards football and become an inspiration for future Black players, much like John Barnes and Cyrille Regis were for him in the eighties and nineties.[14] Jenas's adherence to respectability politics aside, I question whether he would as enthusiastically encourage a Black teacher, TfL worker or NHS worker to rise above racist abuse in order to inspire the next generation of Black public servants. Why should it be any different for Black football players?

FC Porto striker Moussa Marega made headlines in February 2020 by walking off the field after being subjected to monkey chants from the opposing Guimarães fans. What makes Marega's form of protest any less righteous than laconically bearing the abuse in a dignified manner? How much more powerful would it have been if his white teammates had walked off with him in solidarity rather than try to restrain him – a traumatic scene in and of itself – for several minutes?*

There needs to be a dialogue on what being strong in the face of adversity looks like, but more importantly, we need to talk about prioritising our wellbeing over our strength. Recently I've been flirting with the idea of pessimism as an act of empowerment.

Psychologist William James proposed a simple equation for happiness: Happiness = Reality/Expectation. The implication is that, to increase their happiness, an individual has two options – improve their reality or reduce their expectations.[15] We have the power to influence both but only the latter, at least in theory, is completely under our control. In line with this thinking, Gabriele Oettingen, a professor at New York University, has posited that 'pessimism can be a better motivator for achieving goals than optimism'.[16] This might seem counterintuitive, but the rationale lays in the idea that blind optimism tends to create a complacency that reduces our desire and proactiveness in achieving our goals. Per this theory, being pessimistic about the lot of Black people in Britain can actually empower us to take the matter into our own hands. I do not wish to assert that this is Rose's thinking, but if his longing to leave the game is his way of taking control of his happiness in light of his belief that things will not improve in football, then more power to him.

Based on an interview he gave to Channel 4 broadcaster Krishnan Guru-Murthy, George the Poet seems to have arrived

* At the time of writing, there is an ongoing public conversation regarding white complicity in racism in society. The failure of white teammates to stand in solidarity with their Black colleagues is a clear display of this, and warrants further discussion.

at a similar conclusion. He described his lack of faith in the UK government to improve socioeconomic conditions for Black and working-class communities in his lifetime as a 'liberating realisation'.[17] Accepting that national governments appeal to the demands of their majority constituents, who of course are white British citizens, it is unlikely that they will ever prioritise the marginalised concerns of minority communities. The onus is thereby placed on those communities to be innovative and create their own solutions. This dynamic is replicated in the world of football, where advertisers and fans are the main sources of revenue and thus the biggest stakeholders that bodies such as the FA and UEFA serve in order to make profit and ultimately survive. Evidently, neither of these stakeholders has made a particularly strong case for an effective policy to uproot racism in football.

Disengagement

Political movements are often born from the frustrations produced when pessimism hits a critical mass. However, as with any disunited collective, calls for action against racism have been inconsistent, reflecting the diverse contexts and perspectives of those who experience racism. It is the reason why the integrationist politics of segments of the civil rights movement in the USA co-existed with the more radical separatist approach of the Nation of Islam.

Today, the Black diaspora in the West retains remnants of these powerful movements but with some nuance. Admittedly, as a first-generation British-Ghanaian, I find myself seduced to varying degrees by a multitude of approaches, some of which Kehinde Andrews explores in his book *Back to Black*.[18] It's worth noting that Andrews believes that nothing short of a complete upheaval of capitalism in its current form can truly uproot racism. In his estimation, they are deeply intertwined and mutually constitutive. I agree with Andrews, but my interest, at least in the medium term, is less in the immense goal of eradicating racism from humanity. I am more concerned with the many steps needed before that. How can we work towards a healthier, happier, more empowered Black diaspora sooner rather than later?

Parts of my career are intimately tied to the belief that, through educating people about the realities of racism, structural change can take place. Do I believe with the full conviction of my heart that it is true? Not really. Although the liberal guilt of individuals, including those in positions of power, can facilitate initiatives that improve the material situation for some Black people, such changes do not occur quickly enough, broadly enough and definitely not deeply enough. (That is not to say that this work isn't immediately useful.)

Ultimately, to divorce yourself from reliance on these efforts requires just one thing: self-determination (social, economic and political). The wealth of footballers like Danny Rose can afford them at least a degree of this autonomy, but the majority of us do not have this safety net. For most Black people, this would entail pooling our resources through group economics to ensure that we are sufficiently served – especially the most disadvantaged among us – in arenas in which we are typically discriminated against.

Stamford Hill is a two square miles segment of Hackney in North London that houses the largest Hasidic community in Europe. The area is served by institutions including a voluntary emergency response first-aid service (Hatzola), a volunteer community watch group (Shomrim), private schools, a housing development association and an umbrella organisation to represent the community's interests. Could there be self-sufficient

Black communities in the UK akin to the Hasidic community in Stamford Hill?

There are reasons to be sceptical. How do we even define community? Despite the cultural footprint that Black people have made in Britain, we only make up three per cent of the total population, and are dispersed across various urban areas like London and Birmingham. Unlike the Hasidic community in Stamford Hill, which is rooted in ethnic and religious homogeneity, Blackness is loosely based on a broad, shared African heritage but is more largely a political identity. Even in boroughs of London where the highest proportions of Black people live, such as Lewisham, Southwark and Lambeth, the racially integrated make-up of areas, together with the effects of gentrification and the squeezing out of local businesses, make the facilitation of self-sufficient Black communities feel improbable.

Yet the current generation is probably better placed to practise the group economics that precedes self-determination than any before. In an increasingly digitally based economy in which e-commerce is the norm, fintech is growing and education is virtual, movements like Black Pound Day (spearheaded by Swiss, rapper and producer from the legendary So Solid Crew) and Jamii, a discount card and discovery platform for Black British businesses, should give us new impetus for the applicability of group economics in the future.*

* I implore you to check out both on https://blackpoundday.uk and https://lovejamii.com, respectively. I acknowledge that these two interventions primarily benefit Black business owners, but the broader (and more idealistic) point I want to raise is how Black-owned institutions with a specialist interest and understanding of serving Black people can improve access to fundamental services that mainstream institutions have historically failed to equitably provide to Black people in the UK. For example, community-focused interventions like Black Sunday schools or the informal 'paadna' or 'susu' banking systems of older immigrant generations – used to address inequality in education and financial inclusion – can be reinvigorated and made more scalable.

Another angle that is gaining momentum is a reinvigoration of the Back-to-Africa movement, which has been variously popularised during different eras by people including Martin Delany and Marcus Garvey. Given the make-up of Black British society, a large portion of which consists of second-generation immigrants from Africa or the Caribbean, this sentiment is understandable. Many of us still have relatively close connections to our countries of origin through our parents and extended family. When the right-wing voice of the country is screaming 'Go back to your own country' as a rebuttal to criticisms of the Black British experience, the prospect of actually taking this advice on board is starting to look attractive to a growing number. Furthermore, the political and economic uncertainty amplified by the incompetently managed Brexit process (itself a campaign fuelled by racism and xenophobia and funded by racist and xenophobic self-interested individuals) initiated in 2016 and the hostility of the Conservative government showcased by the 2018 Windrush scandal strengthens the appeal.

In the USA, where a political shift to the right has also been pronounced, this bug has similarly caught on during what many Black Americans considered a disappointing Obama administration and a catastrophic Donald Trump presidency. Following the murder of George Floyd, the Back-to-Africa phenomenon was extensively covered by major news media, including the BBC, Al Jazeera, Channel 4 and NBC News. Celebrities of African heritage – notably Senegalese-American Akon and Nigerian-American Jidenna – have long proposed that the African diaspora consider moving to the continent. Jidenna's initial decision to live in Nigeria, or his 'fuck it moment' as he calls it, was born out of necessity, after being evicted by a racist landlord. However, he fully embraces creating a bridge to

Africa as a means for African-Americans to escape an 'abusive relationship' with America.

What I find particularly compelling about Jidenna's stance is that it is pragmatic while also championing Black entitlement, which is something that is rarely done. He calls for the diaspora to develop a global mindset of being both an immigrant *and* a citizen of the USA. Naturally, this idea of demanding what is rightfully yours in the diaspora (financial or otherwise) while also acknowledging you have a home on the continent is also applicable to us in the UK and Europe.[19]

Akon, on the other hand, appeals to business opportunists within the diaspora to seek ways to make money in a burgeoning part of the world to which they have ancestral claims – particularly when Chinese interests, Big Tech and former colonial powers such as Britain and France continue to do so.

In many ways, these perspectives have a ring of romanticisation to them. But to override many of the negative portrayals of Africa in the mass media that have been inherited as a result of colonial and post-colonial depictions of corruption, poverty, black magic and war, maybe an element of fantasy is required. With that said, the propositions of Akon and the like are not fanciful to the point of being unrealistic. The immense skill base, experience and financial resources of the Black diaspora employed on the continent would have an economic and societal impact of incredible magnitude, especially in view of growing domestic middle classes and the infrastructural gaps currently present in the market.

As somebody with skin in the game, the ambitions of my business, Dapaah Chocolates, represents both Jidenna and Akon's frame of thinking. We add value to an abundant African resource – in our case cocoa in Ghana – by producing premium chocolate and selling to affluent markets in the UK and beyond.

By setting up production on the ground, we can create business and employment opportunities for Ghanaian locals and also seek greater profits from an export market which, as young, savvy Londoners with a blossoming brand, we have access to.

Bias aside, a shared understanding of how this dynamic could mutually benefit Africa and its diaspora is probably best exemplified by Ghana. Under the presidency of Nana Akufo-Addo, Ghana has been one of few African nations to formally and proactively push an agenda of creating closer ties with the diaspora. In 2019, 'The Year of Return' initiative saw thousands of Black people living outside the continent return 'back home' to commemorate the 400th anniversary of the first enslaved Africans arriving in the USA. With festivities at their height, and clubs, hotels and beaches overspilling with tourists from across the globe, the highlight was undoubtedly the emotional ceremony in which 126 African-Americans and Afro-Caribbeans were granted Ghanaian citizenship as the lyrics of Osibisa's 'Welcome Home' filled the air at Jubilee House, Ghana's seat of government:

> You've been gone it's an empty home
> Come on back when you're ready to know
> You are always welcome home
> You've been kept on for much too long
> Stand up please and say 'I am free'
> Don't forget you are welcome home
> Come with me
> On this happy trip back to the Promise Land
> All will be happy again

In the following months, the online world witnessed African-American celebrities, politicians and influencers arrive back on American soil cloaked with honorary titles from local chiefs and a new sense of connection to Africa. Some went as far as buying property in the coveted areas on the coasts and in the capital city, Accra.*

We're aware that the privileges that apply in the world of celebrity don't necessarily trickle down to us regular Blacks. For that reason, I understand why the average person in the diaspora remains concerned about how well people from aburokyire (abroad), as Ghanaians would say, are received. For that reason, I find it hugely encouraging that popular YouTube channels like WODE MAYA, boasting millions of views and hundreds of thousands of subscribers, are actively dispelling myths by showcasing the good, bad and ugly sides to various African nations, and speaking with Black people who have already made the transition to the continent to give their honest accounts of the experience.†

This is a trend that I believe will continue for decades to come. For people like my father, returning home was always the plan. Living in the UK was a decision made to build resources, perhaps having initially bought into the idealised image of *Great* Britain as young adults. Thirty years on, he regularly laments the fact that he stayed in the UK as long as he did. As a retired man who has finally relocated back to his homeland, he wonders what life would have been like if he had returned twenty years earlier, as some of his peers did, and utilised his education and skills in an environment where he would

* Beyoncé, Steve Harvey, Samuel L Jackson, and Cardi B were just a few A-list celebrities who visited Ghana for the tourism campaign.

† Other YouTube channels with a similar theme that are growing in popularity include Native Borne, The Only Way Is Ghana, GoBlack2Africa, BlaXit, Diaspora Achievers, Manka & E, Ivy Prospers, Vanessa Kanbi and many more.

have been valued and free from the systemic barriers faced by African immigrants in the UK.

As I watch friends and acquaintances flirt with the idea of a great African exodus to Ghana, Nigeria, Gambia, Sudan, Sierra Leone and Uganda, I wonder if my dad's regrets are a warning for us, for me? Do we let blind optimism that things will improve lull us into a state that keeps us permanently wedded to second-class citizenry, or embrace our pessimism to seek greener pastures where, sure, there will be hurdles, but none related to the happenstance of race. Right now I'm feeling like Rose: give me a few more seasons and I wouldn't mind just walking off the pitch.

A PARALLEL HISTORY OF BLACK MUSLIM FOOTBALLERS

A Parallel History of Black Muslim Footballers

Sanaa Qureshi

In September 2011, the French-born Senegalese international Demba Ba knelt and touched his forehead to the turf at St James' Park after scoring his first goal for Newcastle against Blackburn Rovers. Ba, prostrated in front of the Newcastle faithful, kneeling before God in an act of worship pivotal to how Muslims pray. This small but substantial gesture represented a watershed moment. The presence of Muslim players in the Premier League after this point at once became visible and normal. He finished that particular game with a hat-trick. Ba would go on to score twenty-nine times for Newcastle, his tenure characterised by prolific form in front of goal, and an incredible partnership with fellow Senegalese international Papisse Cissé that eventually earned him a move to a league-chasing Chelsea side in 2013. However, his time at Newcastle was arguably more memorable for the ways in which the practice of his faith was interminably and outwardly wound up with his football.

After the win against Blackburn, Newcastle's then-manager Alan Pardew noted that the start of Ba's career with the Magpies had been sluggish as a direct result of Ramadan, the Muslim holy month when adherents abstain from food and water – among other things – from sunrise to sunset. 'It's difficult for strikers,' he told the assorted press after the match. 'Fasting takes their sharpness away.'[1] Pardew's acknowledgement of the religious month was notable because of the explicit link

When Demba Ba prostrated before God in front of the watching Newcastle supporters in September 2011, he ushered in an era of hyper-visibility for Muslim footballers in the UK.

he drew to Ba's performance, but his words tacitly revealed an additional commitment in the life of a footballer, which otherwise tends to be framed as necessarily single-minded.

Ba's good form continued, and just over a month after his first, he got a second hat-trick against Stoke – the club that he failed a medical for earlier the same year. After the game, he was presented with a joint man of the match award along with his Argentinian teammate, Jonás Gutiérrez. When Ba nudged the bottle of champagne towards his colleague, it looked like a nondescript moment of humility, or tacit appreciation that his success was not his alone. But for Muslim fans, after seeing Ba kneel in prostration towards God on the pitch, the refusal of champagne became another moment in which they could see themselves.

In the final weeks of the 2020–21 Premier League season, Leicester City were taking on Crystal Palace at the King Power Stadium when, approximately thirty minutes into the game, both teams paused for Leicester's French international Wesley Fofana and Palace's Senegalese midfielder, Cheikhou Kouyaté to open their fast. It was midway through the holy month of Ramadan and the first time in Premier League history that both teams had agreed with the referee before the game that play would temporarily cease for players to eat and drink. Referee Graham Scott paused the game, Palace goalkeeper Vicente Guaita delayed his goal kick and both Fofana and Kouyaté went to the sidelines. After the game, Fofana publicly thanked the Premier League, Crystal Palace, Guaita and his Leicester City teammates for their support. The moment was covered extensively by mainstream football media.

This was not the first time a footballer had opened their fast during a Premier League football match, nor would it be the last time that season (Fofana was seen doing so a few times). The significance of the occasion was both the open acknowledgement of what happened and the desire to embed the act into the ebb and flow of the ninety minutes. Ramadan is an inherently communal month, during which Muslims all over the world follow the same patterns of fasting, of prayer and of submission. The decision to stop the game transformed what had previously been a personal moment, observed and noted by Muslim football fans following the same routines, into a decidedly public one.

In stark contrast to Pardew a decade earlier, Fofana's manager, Brendan Rodgers, commented positively on his young defender's commitment to his faith by highlighting the continued quality of his contribution during the holy month while also opting to protect him where appropriate. During a 3–0 win against West Bromwich Albion, Rodgers substituted Fofana at the hour mark. After the game he was asked about whether this decision was down to injury:

> He's fine. He's a young player in the middle of Ramadan, so he's obviously not eating during the day. It's absolutely remarkable. If you think of his performance at the weekend in an FA Cup semi-final, where he hasn't eaten all day, and then he had his first taste of food with fifteen minutes to go, and then the same today, with the 8pm kick off, he's not eaten all day or drank, and he can still perform to that level. It was just one where I thought if I could get him off, then he could get some food into him on the bench, and just protect him a little bit.

After the journalist expresses awe at the devotion to his faith, Rodgers continues:

> I've worked with lots of players with similar devotion to their faiths and what it does is, for a lot of the guys it gives them strength. He's finding an incredible strength to play continuously and train while ... in Ramadan. He's a special talent and a big player for us.[2]

//

There was a time before it was common to see Premier League footballers hold their hands together in prayer while mouthing 'Ayatul-Kursi'* before kick-off, when the sight of a

* Ayatul Kursi is also known as the Throne Verse. It is the 255th verse of the second chapter of the Quran. The verse is widely memorised and often recited to ward off evil and misfortune.

footballer on their knees after a goal would be read as kissing the turf and nothing more. There was a time before stories of players praying with a local congregation filtered through Twitter and into WhatsApp messages, before it was possible to see which footballers from rival clubs spent the off-season completing the sacred pilgrimage to Mecca together. Scraps of information were pieced together through word of mouth, and all that was understood about their lives in relation to their faith was either witnessed during games, or discovered via media revelation laden with bias and refracted through the perennially myopic white gaze.

To find a measure of convergence between what was taking place within the private homes of Muslims and the public lives of the players they so deeply beloved and adored was to actively seek it out, to share it among family and friends, and to hold it close as the realities of being a Black Muslim in Britain threatened the joys of simple unadulterated fandom. What underpins this essay is an exploration of that affection through conversations that open up the impact Black Muslim footballers have on Black Muslim fans, and – by extension – these fans' interactions with the sport they love and the footballers they adore, and their own relationships with their faith.

//

In the inaugural season of the Premier League, Tottenham Hotspur's Spanish midfielder Mohamed Alí Amar, more commonly known as Nayim, was the only known Muslim playing at the highest level in England. Although there is no definitive way to collate and parse this data, over the following years, a smattering of Muslim footballers from abroad joined clubs throughout England, including Nii Lamptey, Moussa Saïb and

Ibrahima Bakayoko. By the end of the nineties, this number was arguably in the double figures – retrospective confirmation of the faiths of foreign footballers who may not have had a huge impact in the Premier League remains tricky. Setting aside the fact that the internet did not exist in the same way that it does now, there was no impetus to understand the faith of individual footballers, partly because the commercial benefits of appealing specifically to Muslims, or people of faith, were yet to be articulated, but perhaps also because Muslims cut across various races, ethnicities and migration patterns and so constituted an indistinct demographic. However, as the stature of the Premier League evolved and grew in the noughties, it benefited from a more global approach to recruitment and marketing and it soon became clear that this geographically expansive fandom was beginning to open up football culture.

A short film produced for the BBC in 2013 titled *The Muslim Premier League*[3] followed Ali Al-Habsi, a critical member of the Wigan squad that won the FA Cup that same year, and examined the presence and influence of Muslim footballers on English football's greatest stage. To acknowledge the outsized impact of Muslims in that particular moment, the narrator, Colin Murray, opens the film by telling us that: 'Twenty years ago there were no Muslim players in the English Premier League.' This statement is designed to announce the relevance of what we're about to see, but it also simultaneously skims over the Muslim footballers that played in England in the intervening years. The appetite to discover who these individuals were and how they were received and understood by fans developed finally when celebratory prostrations were too prevalent to ignore, and man of the match champagne bottles had been politely refused by the same player – Manchester City midfielder Yaya Touré – too frequently. In this sense, there are clearly two histories of Muslim footballers in the Premier League – an 'official' history that can be verified, recorded and tethered to some of the most successful imports English football has housed, and a second history, which has been collected by fans. This alternative history is unverified and largely unwritten, and is instead shared as rumour and informed by Google deep-dives.

I spoke to a number of Black Muslim football fans about the players they admired, and delved into how their fandoms had been shaped by Black Muslim footballers who have plied their trade in the Premier League. Many of the fans I spoke with articulated how this alternative history had indelibly influenced their fandom, but not necessarily with regards to the teams they supported and their associated histories. Patterns and legacies of fandom often follow similar lines – a local connection, familial persuasion or an affinity for a club's playing style. This was not broadly different for the fans I spoke with. However, these lines seemed to diverge when it came to following the fortunes of Muslim players. In this instance, fans held emotional space for players at other clubs or in other leagues. For Black Muslims raised in Britain, there seemed to be no conflict in rooting for someone like Touré, or Sadio Mané, or to hope for longevity and success for N'Golo Kanté, whichever club they supported. It was considered integral to the holistic experience of both fandom and football to root for anyone who could embody, even for a moment, what it feels like to be a Black Muslim in Britain today.

Through analysing the cultural and social relevance of the mostly Black Muslim footballers through the eyes of white fans and terrace chants, manager Sam Allardyce and *Times* football writer Henry Winter offered a layman's perspective (and baseless optimism) in *The Muslim Premier League* and unintentionally convey precisely where football culture has been stuck for the longest time. When asked about the health benefits of Muslim players abstaining from alcohol, Allardyce replied, 'They still go to the nightclubs – don't worry about that.' It's clear that the mainstream assessment of Islam at the time was fixated on terrorism – either the racist associations freely thrown about by an openly hostile media, or an aggressive desire to repudiate this link through the Good Muslims–Bad Muslims paradigm.

Alongside this extremely base duality, which continues to occupy much of the discourse about Muslims, the standard image of a British Muslim is nearly always South Asian, to the continued detriment of Black Muslims. The film closes out on a community football session led by Zesh Rehman, the first British Asian to start a Premier League match, where teenage boys and young men are playing under floodlights and a question is asked about the possibility of seeing a Muslim footballer pull on an England shirt for a full international debut. Rehman responds: 'When the day comes when a British Asian kid plays for England, it'll be massive in terms of integration and opening up the mind-sets of people a lot more because if [there's] one thing that can create harmony, it's football.' It may have been a slip of the tongue, or a truism spouted through muscle memory, as Rehman reflected on his own experiences, but his default understanding of a Muslim footballer as South Asian laid bare the challenge presented to Black British Muslims by a footballing culture that still struggles to make space for and understand them.

When the cultural impact of Black people in Britain has been so enormous, and the professional, technical and artistic impact of Black Muslim footballers in Britain is becoming equally significant, it seems a curious oversight that this doesn't form a more critical part of studies of football fandom, the construction of British identity or the British Muslim experience. Nevertheless, the vastness of football ensures it remains uniquely placed to open up and unpack these questions of identity and belonging, particularly within the heaving multiplicities of fandom. The documentary ends on a saccharine note of hope, a self-serving battle cry of professional football's meritocracy – 'The best will inevitably make it' – but eight years on, and with a Muslim population of almost 3 million in England, we're all still waiting for the one.

Who do exist, however, are those who came from elsewhere and maybe made it here, or made it after they left, or prepared the ground for others. Through the course of many long, detailed conversations, I was able to start appreciating the myriad ways individual footballers have enhanced the experience of Black British Muslim fans and zoomed in on their own relationship with God.

//

Isaaq Suleiman, a 22-year-old Tottenham fan who has lived in London his whole life, began his fandom with a desire to look into the team his elder brother, an Arsenal fan, disliked. It was a happy coincidence that the first Muslim footballer he heard of was Frédéric Kanouté, even though Isaaq was too young to remember Kanouté's time in the Premier League in the early 2000s. 'When he left Sevilla, it was a really big deal,' Isaaq told me. 'His talent sometimes gets lost in his activism but he was so talented.' The reverence in which the now-retired Kanouté is held as both a technically gifted footballer and righteous man by Black Muslim football fans in Britain is fascinating, because much of the prevailing mythology around him is born of incidents and stories that took place once he'd left England. If anything, the depth of this mythology is intensified further because there are so few discernible memories of his influence on Premier League games. In this sense, his impact on British Muslims is unencumbered by the specificity of the British experience, and strengthened by the thread holding together Muslim football fans around the world. The importance of Kanouté to Muslim football fans in Britain is less about what he did while here, and more about their pride that he was here in the first place.

The timing of Kanouté's career was also significant, as it coincided with the era before overexposure on social media. During this period, international footballers who gained popularity while playing in the Premier League were able to create and sustain a mythology more potent than their successors. Of course, it's easier to put Black Muslims from this generation on a pedestal: the absence of visible, relatable role models within British football opened up the space to pass around and elevate the stories of those who did exist, like Kanouté. Ali Mohammed, a Liverpool fan from London, was keen to point out that there was also very little known about Kanouté's life, or the practice of his faith outside the incidents everyone seemed to talk about: 'It's not like he had an Instagram to share more about himself, so whatever he did felt exaggerated because that's all we knew about him.' And so, despite his relatively minimal playing time in the Premier League, Kanouté's legacy continues to be profound. The half-life of his actions extend farther than his career and his footballing achievements, and much farther than his time in Britain.

After signing from fellow London side West Ham, Kanouté found himself bizarrely maligned by Jacques Santini and club administrators at Tottenham, who questioned his eligibility to represent Mali and attempted to block his international clearance when he was selected to form part of the 2004 African

Cup of Nations squad.[4] A revolving door of managers and subsequent indifferent playing form at Tottenham caused his career in the Premier League to stutter and stall. It was at Sevilla, the club he joined in 2005, that Kanouté settled into an environment that would both define his career and fortify the perception of him that would outlive his playing days. In January 2009, during Operation Cast Lead, an Israeli military assault on the Gaza Strip, Kanouté lifted his shirt after scoring in a cup tie against Deportivo La Coruña to display a message of solidarity with the Palestinian people. This moment remains significant for the fans I spoke to. It is a fixed point of pride for Muslims that a professional footballer demonstrated in practice what it means to be part of a global Ummah

In January 2009, during Operation Cast Lead, an Israeli military assault on the Gaza Strip, Frédéric Kanouté lifted his shirt after scoring in a cup tie against Deportivo La Coruña to display a message of solidarity with the Palestinian people.

(an Arabic word that means community and is often used to mean the collective community of Muslims) and was willing to extend his contribution to the world beyond his ability to play football.

Kanouté continued to embody the qualities he is now renowned for by supporting jailed Palestinian footballer Mahmoud Sarsak and making a considerable contribution to the restoration of the local temporary mosque in Seville – and when the city's Muslim population began to outgrow that modest building, he helped to fundraise the construction of the first purpose-built mosque in the city for 700 years. Although the expression of support and solidarity with Palestine is not an exclusively Islamic action, all the individuals I interviewed discussed how Palestinian activism defined how their political and Islamic educational journeys combined. As Abdul-Khalid Afolabi, a Manchester United fan from London, told me, 'It was incredible to see a professional footballer hold the same ideals,' to see a footballer 'embody the Muslim ideal.'

In 2006, Kanouté famously refused to wear a betting sponsor on his shirt. This decision drew a clear line between the business of football and the practice of his faith. Sevilla's willingness to understand and work with Kanouté – who'd become an integral part of the team – illustrated the growing influence of Muslim footballers on the upper echelons of the professional leagues. Ali suggested that Kanouté's stance would have probably encouraged Papiss Cissé when he spoke out in 2013 about Newcastle's then-sponsor, payday loans company Wonga. 'That's the best kind of legacy to leave, to help someone else fight injustice,' he told me.

In a December 2020 appearance on Spanish football journalist Guillem Balagué's *Pure Football Podcast*, Kanouté was asked a series of probing questions, which caused him to open up about the fundamental role faith plays in his life. First, quite incredulously, Balagué asked Kanouté if he believes in God, to which Kanouté replied:

> Yes, definitely. I mean, 100 per cent. It is part of my life, who I am, especially since I reverted to Islam in my early twenties. My relationship with God has been the engine of my life, of my behaviour, of my social relationships. It's a way of life. More than a religion for me, it's a way of life, and a way to connect with God and connect with other people.[5]

Balagué seemed unable to comprehend what this meant, using clumsy terms to try and redefine or repackage the certainty through which Kanouté discussed the most important thing in his life. Evident in this exchange is the fact that the biggest and most influential football journalists in world football are woefully ill-equipped to discuss and appreciate what drives the people they have made careers out of following, and how to contemplate the esteem with which players like Kanouté are held. Abdul-Khalid articulated Kanouté's influence perfectly when he told me that Kanouté showed Muslims how to pursue a career, how to succeed while holding God at the centre of it all, and how to ensure your legacy in this world, often referred to as Sadaqah Jariyah (an Arabic term for a long-term act of kindness that continues after you have passed away), can be your actions and not just your work.

The impact of Kanouté's activism felt particularly poignant when Leicester City – in front of 21,000 spectators, the largest crown since the beginning of the COVID-19 pandemic – defeated Chelsea 1–0 to become FA Cup champions in May, 2021. The final took place on 15 May, Nakba Day, a commemoration of the forcible and violent displacement of Palestinians in 1948 when Israel was created, amid renewed attacks across occupied Palestinian territories.

That same day, protests took place around the world in solidarity with Palestinians suffering through the latest round of Israeli military escalation in their ongoing, brutal occupation. As the Leicester players celebrated on pitch after the match, Hamza Choudhury, a Muslim Bangladeshi-Grenadian midfielder who came through the Leicester City Academy and represented England at under-21 level, found a spectator in the crowd with a Palestine flag and wrapped it around his body as he collected his winners medal.

Choudhury then held the flag alongside Wesley Fofana, both players posing for a photo while publicly expressing solidarity with Palestinians on the biggest day of their careers thus far. Images of the players were shared across social media, inspiring predictable opprobrium from Zionists but widespread support among those demanding freedom for Palestine. Their spontaneous decision helped to flesh out a line from Kanouté directly through to these two Black, Muslim footballers, and simultaneously connected them to a global movement of support. It was difficult not to feel heartened.

//

As Kanouté departed the Premier League for Sevilla in 2005, Nathan Ellington entered it with West Brom, making his debut for the club that August. In his previous season at Wigan, the striker had helped the club achieve promotion to the Premier League, featuring in the Championship team of the season. At the time of his arrival, Ellington was the only known Black British Muslim playing in the Premier League. Ellington, who was born a Christian and raised in Bradford,

Hamza Choudhury brandishes the flag of Palestine after Leicester City's 2021 FA Cup win over Chelsea.

had an early career in line with the trajectories of most home-grown players who make their way through the lower leagues. Ellington's journey to Islam is more complex than cursory internet searches throw up, and through a wide-ranging conversation with him, it became clear that his challenges foreshadowed many of the changes that would later come about in the top tiers of English football as a result of prominent overseas Muslim players.

According to his Wikipedia page, Ellington converted to marry his Muslim wife. However, the reality offers a much more interesting and thoughtful insight into the potential of shared faith to build active community, and the perception of Islam in mainstream society, particularly within football. Ellington's older brother converted to Islam before him, and was the route through which he was initially exposed to the practical elements of the faith before understanding the spiritual. Through personal investigation on the internet and extensive, far-reaching conversations with friends, Ellington methodically worked through questions he had – How did the Qur'an come to be? What does Jesus mean to Muslims? – slowly pulling together a method to live that became fundamental to him. Although the impetus for his exploration may have been his partner, Ellington emphasises that his desire to believe foregrounded his journey. His personal moment of revelation arrived via a YouTube video on science and Islam, a fact that reinforces the breadth of the research he undertook.

Recalling the moment, he emphasised that it was an intangible moment of clarity that changed him: 'I went from someone that did not believe in God to someone that did, immediately.' It was during his best season as a professional footballer that Ellington converted to Islam. With his sister-in-law present, he took the Shahadah, an Islamic creed and the basis of Islamic belief. At that moment, after many months of learning and delving, there was no seismic shift. Instead of it feeling like a monumental occasion, Ellington's formal acceptance of Islam, in his words, 'just felt like who I'd been all along'.

Speaking to Ellington now, it's obvious that he arrived in the Premier League at a time before it was clear how to carefully and considerately work with Muslim footballers. Instead, they were expected to conform to its cultural rigidities. It was 'not unusual' for his peers to 'go out and party, from after training until the next day', something which Ellington had never been interested in. From the outside, it might have seemed like he wasn't very engaged in his career as a professional footballer because he spent so much of his down time shying away from the activities most other footballers engaged in at the time. 'I would rather learn something about Islam than play cards,' he admitted sweetly.

There's a widely held assumption that English football is a meritocracy, or that talent remains the most critical currency. But there's only so much that raw talent can do in the face of structural racism or deep-rooted inequality. While Ellington was playing, it was difficult to access halal meat, or for his colleagues and coaches to understand the significance of Ramadan (other than as a nuisance to the football season). He was accused by managers of being distracted by prayer before he'd actually even learnt how to do so, which he committed to over a period of years, learning Arabic slowly.

Being born a Muslim and finding the faith later in life are two very different experiences. Ellington had to navigate the earliest years of his newfound faith battling the deep-seated misconceptions of those around him, while simultaneously still learning about everything that being a Muslim encompassed. That it was seemingly so easy for managers to dismiss Ellington's difficult patches as being related to or caused by his faith speaks both to the ignorance at the time and, equally, to the absence of the critical mass of Muslim footballers that would come half a decade later.

Nathan Ellington, pictured in action for West Brom, played at a time when managers were largely ignorant of his faith. He helped to set up the Association of Muslim Footballers in 2012 as a way of ensuring that future generations coming through the English football leagues would be supported in ways he wasn't.

Despite the challenges, Ellington spoke with an envious conviction about his journey to and with Islam. The setbacks he suffered as his career should have been peaking only strengthened his resolve, his relationship with God holding him together while club and managerial changes conspired against him. The friendships he developed with Diomansy Kamara (at West Bromwich Albion) and Mamady Sidibé (at Stoke City), bonds that still hold strong today, enabled Ellington to find his feet as a practising Muslim footballer. All based in the Midlands, Kamara and Sidibé would meet Ellington at

Birmingham Central Mosque for prayer when their schedules allowed, providing him with camaraderie and comfort in a league hostile to difference. This experience drove Ellington to build something for younger players that could last. He helped to set up the Association of Muslim Footballers in 2012 as a way of ensuring the future generation coming through the English football leagues would be supported to make time for prayer should they need it, access the appropriate catering and tangibly feel the benefits of belonging to an Ummah.

It was the community created among key first-team Muslim footballers at Newcastle United in 2013 that led to the installation of a multi-faith prayer room at St James' Park, an act that ensured their faith was acknowledged as a central part of their lives. Throughout all the conversations I had, this was a theme that reappeared often. Isaaq spoke about how uplifting it is to see Muslim footballers from across the league completing the pilgrimage, or praying Jummah (special congregational prayers that take place every Friday) in the same congregation. This is made possible through social media and the desire of the footballers to actively share their faith and devotion with the world. These depictions of brotherhood between individuals who may otherwise be competing against each other provide fans like Isaaq and Ali with an image that mirrors what they may have in their own lives, and, as Ali told me, 'an aspiration for who we want to continue to be'.

Sharmaarke Ali Adan, a Huddersfield Town fan, went into more detail: 'Seeing [Paul] Pogba and [Kurt] Zouma doing Umrah felt so good. It strengthens your own faith because it provides more motivation for you to do that, and to emulate them.' Like other respondents, Shaarmarke reiterated how uplifting it is to see world-famous, wealthy footballers engaging in the same rituals as other Muslims.

While all the interviewees had come across the Association of Muslim Footballers, only one, Ali, had a memory of Ellington as a Black, British, Muslim footballer who had played at the highest level. But Ellington is clear about his legacy, even if his name isn't associated with it: 'There are more opportunities and openings for footballers today. Things are more integrated and they can be open about their beliefs. It's important they can do that now.'

//

Understanding and unpacking the impact of Black Muslim footballers on fans is as much about acknowledging the messiness of memory and fandom as it is recognising how the hyper-white British media and footballing establishment have, through targeting their vitriol at particular individuals, inadvertently built heroes for British Muslims. Almost everyone I spoke with told me how important Manchester United and France midfielder Paul Pogba had become as a prominent Black Muslim footballer playing in the Premier League precisely because he had been so ostracised for his clothing, hair choices and attitude. His detractors often claim these things impacted his 'focus' – a trope often levelled at Black footballers in general. Tottenham fan Isaaq still remembers watching Manchester City take on United at the Etihad in 2018 via a stream on his phone while he attended a wedding: 'At half-time, [Graeme] Souness was giving him [Pogba] so much shit and he comes out in the second half and kills it. They only won 3–2 because of him.'

In this instance, the maligning that took place at the hands of the largely white, largely male football media underscored how, despite their singular achievements within the sport, footballers like Pogba continue to feel like underdogs. As Ali articulated,

'When you see someone who's won loads of trophies in Italy and a World Cup still having his seriousness doubted you just think, *What more does he have to do?*' Isaaq bluntly told me that Pogba should leave United 'so he can thrive' without the unfair glare of the English press. This feeling of being under-appreciated was shared across the interviewees, who saw an element of their experiences in how Pogba had been treated – needing to overcome persistent questions about attitude or commitment were littered throughout the conversations. But equally, they revelled in Pogba's unmistakable brilliance, and the moments of lightness that help to shape him as a whole individual.

Fans who live in Manchester relay stories of Pogba visiting Didsbury Mosque, praying shoulder to shoulder with the Muslim congregation in the local community. This perception of humility is critical in forging connections with the Black Muslim footballers whose lives resonate most deeply with fans. Sprinkled throughout all of the conversations I had were anecdotes – some personal, some passed on, some now considered legitimate folklore – of footballers practising their faith within the community and how meaningful these instances continue to be.

The now-infamous story of Chelsea midfielder and France international N'Golo Kanté missing his Eurostar train from London to Paris, finding a local mosque to say his prayers and winding up playing *FIFA* at the home of an Arsenal fan was relayed to me in every single interview. For one person, it was Kanté's desire to pray, his unwavering commitment to this particular tenet of the faith that stood out. For another, it was observing how an Ummah can function at its most mundane, and most wonderful. Speaking to the BBC, Badlur Rahman Jalil, the fan who invited Kanté home, explained, 'It's Islamic teaching to invite guests to your house for dinner, so I asked him,' distilling in very simple terms an etiquette central to Islam.[6]

While the mainstream view perceived Kanté spending an evening eating, playing video games and catching up on highlights with strangers as mildly absurd or unlikely, to Muslims, this was merely a representation of the player embracing the invisible thread tying each of us together as an Ummah. As Ali told me, 'Kanté was just doing what we'd been raised to do – to be polite, to accept sincere invitations, to eat alongside the people we pray with.' But his ability to combine these things with a remarkable football career among the excesses of wealth and fame surrounding him injected a very tender sincerity into how he continues to be regarded and held up.

Liverpool and Senegal's Sadio Mané was similarly discussed with a great deal of affection, with Isaaq sharing each of the stories he'd heard about Mané in the local mosque – from helping an elderly man do Wudu (the Islamic procedure of cleansing parts of the body in preparation for prayer), to cleaning the facilities with volunteers, to simply being an active member of the congregation. Each video released seemed to have been met by consternation from the Senegalese footballer, who was understandably keen to maintain some semblance of privacy. But Isaaq was grateful to have glanced at these snippets: 'I was taught to do the same thing by my mother – you gotta help your elders. I know Mané was angry the video was released but … it was so nice to see.' Similarly, Ali told me how these stories showed other Muslims how to fully embody the faith, even in a place like Britain where, 'It can feel like it's easier to flatten parts of your identity, especially in football, where the prevailing culture can be obnoxious, territorial and loud.'

Mané's importance as a Black Muslim footballer in his local community is matched by what he's accomplished on the pitch, as a player and as a symbol for Muslims around the world. Ali discussed how the contribution of Mané alongside Mohamed Salah has been so integral not just to the success of Liverpool but also specifically to the goodwill generated around the club outside its own fanbase. In an interview with Channel 4's Krishnan Guru-Murthy referencing the infamous Salah chant – 'If he's good enough for you, he's good enough for me. If he scores another few, then I'll be Muslim too' – that threatened to convert a large portion of the Kop to Islam, Liverpool manager Jürgen Klopp revealed allowances he had made to pre-match scheduling in order to enable the Muslim contingent of the squad to complete rituals important to them.[7] For Sharmaarke, learning that Mané took to the pitch having done his Wudu resulted in a huge part of his identity feeling strangely vindicated.

As a keen recreational footballer, Sharmaarke always makes dua (a prayer of request made directly to God) before playing football, whether five-a-side or eleven-a-side, and at moments of acute frustration finds himself returning to God:

> If I'm having a bad game or feel like I'm off, if there's a chance to pause, I'll whisper a prayer to myself, or ask God to help me improve, but I always felt like I was taking it too seriously, or that I shouldn't be calling on God during a pointless game of football.

Seeing that players like Mané had integrated similar rituals into their game helped Sharmaarke feel a sense of kinship but also, crucially, reminded him that these were all ways of staying close to God and to keeping faith at the heart of everything. This resonated with Idiris Sheikhnur, a 26-year-old Manchester United fan born and raised in the city. When discussing seeing players make dua before a game, or prostrate, he remarked that it was a sign of a 'communal spirit – it's that feeling of praying next to a brother you don't know but you're still connected to through this religion. It gives people an identity and strength.'

When Mané and Salah prostrate after they score, in celebration of their achievements, it prompts Sharmaarke to also remember God in the happy moments, as well as during the adverse ones. It was through discussing moments of joy that Yaya Touré became a key part of my conversations, with each of the interviewees recognising the immense contribution he made both as one of the best midfielders the Premier League has ever seen and by complicating the racist binary that commonly traps Black footballers between humble and arrogant. Idiris spoke at length about what Touré had meant to his younger sibling, encouraging him to nurture loving and lasting bonds with the club he supports – Manchester City. He remembers watching his little brother in the moment City first won the title, how, through observing and supporting Touré, he became a dedicated fan.

Idiris was keen to emphasise that, as a Black Muslim, it was possible with Touré to appreciate his brilliance as a footballer while empathising equally with how he was treated by the wider footballing community, who perhaps didn't give him the respect he was owed. For Ali, Touré embodied the adage of Black people needing to work twice as hard for recognition, leading to 'the defining central midfielder of a generation being excluded from conversations that in reality should have only been about him'. But Idiris was keen to build on this and told me that, although these parallels may have resonated for him and lots of other Black people, he also found great strength in Touré's goofiness, and his good humour: 'He often came across like a funny immigrant parent – very lovable.'

Touré was also instrumental in changing the post-match procedure for players who were awarded man of the match. He was winning the award so often – and refusing the champagne every time – that Barclays (the sponsors of the Premier League) eventually moved on from giving professional footballers alcohol, instead settling on a trophy. For Idiris and Ali, this was a huge feat. Touré's individual brilliance had democratised an award, a part of footballing culture that had, through its centring of alcohol, always felt hostile to Muslims. Furthermore, Touré also personified for them the hopes and dreams of a continent, showing millions of people the breadth of possibility.

It was via discussions of symbolism that many of the interviewees brought up players doing Sujud, the act of prostrating to God, and soon we ended up talking about Demba Ba again. For a footballer who only spent three and a half years in the Premier League, his impact as a Black Muslim has been profound. Alongside scoring at a blistering rate, Ba was known to lead his fellow Muslim teammates at Newcastle, including Papiss Cissé, Cheick Tioté and Hatem Ben Arfa, in prayer. His was the first name mentioned when I asked Ibrahim Sudi, an Arsenal fan from London, about what it meant to see Black Muslim footballers in the sport he'd loved his whole life. 'I still remember Demba Ba prostrating with Cissé and thinking *Damn – if they're Muslim there must be many more Muslims around*.' This sentiment was echoed by Abdul-Khalid, who told me that outward displays of worship made the connection between himself and individual footballers feel much stronger and much more real:

> I saw players like me. I've loved football since I was young and played it but ... I thought it might not be the place for

me, partly because of the racism but the lad culture too. But nowadays players are proud of where they come from and they aren't afraid to say prayers or thank God.

//

Footballers like Demba Ba have been able to cultivate and sustain this affection from fans long after their time in the Premier League has ended partly due to public pronouncements of faith, but equally critically – moments of levity and light. The Senegalese striker's fondness for a French strawberry cordial that he referred to as a syrup was mentioned in my conversations as often as Ba's celebratory prostration. It was clear from each interviewee that, while a shared faith remains the foremost tie that binds them to these footballers, the totality of their appeal is not limited to Islam, but extends to their exuberance, their talent, their joy, their strange habits and their expressions of brotherhood.

In order to find out the number of Muslim footballers currently playing in the Premier League, you would need to combine names and suggestions from various websites and match them up to squad lists and individual social media profiles. Considering the impact that Black Muslim footballers have had on Black Muslims, a group routinely erased from representations of the British Muslim experience, it feels especially chastening that this archive is not yet being built, or these experiences charted.

The Premier League has made an unimaginable amount of money through the commodification of the diversity of talent that comes to this country to play professional football. They've done this without ever trying to understand how this diversity has shifted and developed fandoms, and how it has enabled a new generation of football fans to find something more meaningful in the ninety minutes. The most illuminating and sometimes surprising part of this series of discussions was parsing why certain footballers had become so revered, why they had cult status for Muslims, and why the faith of particular individuals was remembered more than others. So much of it returned to what is seen reflected back to fans, which is not unlike football fandom more broadly. We watch football to see people do things we can't do, to play a game we may innately understand but in all likelihood can never sufficiently replicate or emulate. The power of recognition is immense.

For the respondents, they saw their immigrant uncle, their activist cousin and the resident joker of their friendship group. They also saw better versions of themselves, versions that remembered to thank God at moments of joy as well as seeking His guidance at moments of turmoil. Versions that were always proud of their Blackness and their faith, that sought to put more good in the world. Versions that continued to find joy in football. Instead of an official record, what we have is a parallel history, carried among fans who have watched the sport they love closer than anyone else. And the sanctity of what they've seen and felt is richer for its intimacy, for its smallness, because that's where all the meaning lives for them.

SOUTH LONDON SOIL

South London Soil

Aniefiok 'Neef' Ekpoudom

In the beginning I remember Saturday training sessions on the rec, remember sprawling green fields and the rolling hill we climbed like a mountain. I remember Golas moulded around size four feet and metal studs screwed into Umbro soles. Mesh bibs and Mitre footballs. Part-time coaches and passing drills.

More than two decades have passed. I am almost twenty-nine now. But I still remember how things were back then. How they started. How we gathered in numbers on crisp Saturday mornings, seven-year-olds cut loose on Lewisham playing greens. We were young kids pulled into a sport handed down through the local family network, a Lewisham tradition slowly becoming our own, the crossfade of football and Saturday mornings bending and shifting into ritual. Every generation just following the last.

I still remember those weekends, still see the grass, still see the rise we climbed like Everest, the pitches where we were baptised. I still remember Hilly Fields. I still remember South London.

Hillyfielders FC was my childhood football club. Hilly Fields was where I played my first game. Thirty acres of open grass and thick tree lining and tennis courts, a sprawling grass junction in the Blue Borough, Brockley and Ladywell and Lewisham Central quietly lapping at its sea green shores. It is wide parkland carved into residential sprawl, besieged by blanket rows of Victorian and terraced housing. It is the jewel of a concrete town, raised a few hundred feet above sea level. From our Everest you can stare down towards the skyscrapers of the city skyline and see steel mountains rising from the earth, glistening along a glass-panelled shorefront.

Sometime in the late nineties, Ron Bell, a local coach and the uncle of a boy from our estate, began running training sessions, gathering flocks of South London infants on preserved public park. Young boys dragged into ritual by fathers who dreamed of one day seeing the family name printed on Premier League jerseys. We found our feet on that turf, swung skinny legs at size 3 footballs, scampered across the short grass, chased elusive low balls towards plastic goalposts, broke in our new arena.

But we were not the first. There were other Black boys in other decades who came before us, kids who stumbled to their feet on the same turf we called our own. Stare back across years and you can trace origin stories, track valley streams back to mountain springs and gather how a people have bent and pulled through time, readied the soil for a new generation to flow into its own singular existence. Fingerprints of the past in our DNA. Old blood in a new world.

A Hilly Fields FC played these grounds through the football seasons of the sixties and seventies, with a few solitary Black faces speckled among the traditional team photos on archived club websites. A boy named Don Fields and another named Delroy Richards, a Vic Banton and an Albert St Clair: Black kids with tight afros, South London footballers frozen in time. Ian Wright played these fields in the late sixties too, before Palace, before Arsenal and England, before *179 Just Done It* and his jersey pulled over his face at Highbury. 'I never lost a game playing in Hilly Fields,' he once said. 'Never lost a game.'[1]

Footballers are symbols, their existence on the public stage an illustration of shifting social and economic dynamics, of immigration and new communities that have taken root. I was born during a time when Lewisham and South London had been imposing their will on British football. The early nineties, a time when David Rocastle had come out of the Honor Oak Estate in Brockley, and Ian Wright had come with him. The Wallace brothers: Danny, Rod and Ray out of Deptford in the north of the borough, who went on to play for Southampton together, Rod winning the old First Division with Leeds in the year before it became the Premier League. The left-back Chris Powell and the striker Kevin Campbell. Midfielders Michael Thomas and Paul Davis who played with Rocastle through Arsenal's golden period in the late eighties and early nineties.

Their collective presence in the Football League was an indicator of something more, of how things were in South

(From L–R) Kevin Campbell, Michael Thomas, David Rocastle and Paul Davis celebrate winning the 1991 First Division title. All four men are South Londoners.

London, how things are, how they will be. Those players I had come to know as a young boy, Ian Wright the record-breaker and Kevin Campbell in Everton blue, were collective illustrations of the shifting dynamics and migrations at work in the corners south of the Thames.

How a community comes to congregate and assemble in a space, a road, a borough, a city often remains unwritten. These stories lie in the personal and private folklores that echo behind the sealed walls of home, in oral histories that never reach official records. And so, while there is no definitive reason as to why Black communities wandered south into the Blue Borough, in the 'Lewisham Characterisation Study' published by Lewisham Council in 2019, the suggestion is that Black immigrants arrived in the borough from the Caribbean throughout the sixties, searching for work in hospitals and on the railways.

James Leighton's book *Rocky: The Tears and Triumphs of David Rocastle* alludes to the same, adding factory work and jobs at the docks to the motivations that pulled Black immigrants south.[2] Rocastle's mother Linda worked in Greenwich Hospital; his father Leslie worked in the local factories. Both were among a steady wave of Black settlers carving their presence into South London rock. In *Rocky*, the Honor Oak Estate of the seventies is portrayed as a Caribbean enclave, reminiscent of lost home countries in sight, sound and smell. Players like Rocastle, with Grenada and Trinidad in his heritage, are a signpost of that early migration, the stories of a people who came from elsewhere.

African immigrants began to settle en masse in South London from the eighties. My parents drifted in from Nigeria and Cameroon, as did my godparents, and my brother's godparents too. When I arrived at Lewisham Hospital in the summer of '92, and still when I became aware of football a few years later, Wright was centre stage. Fathers like mine, strangers in a new country who were fluent in football's universal tongue but wary of a hostile time on British terraces, were drawn to Wright and Arsenal and the club's rolling Black contingent out of South London.

And so, in those early years, I remember a borough and a home bristling with pride for its golden son. Nobody told you that he was from around here. You knew by instinct. I watched him play in my highchair. His name was painted on the walls, his essence infused into the water. I knew. My brother knew. My parents knew. My neighbours knew. This was his ground zero, and every young kid from that time has an Ian Wright story they are ready to repeat, encounters told and retold by parents like mine until the details have become concrete.

There was the school competition I won in Year 1 a few weeks after Wright broke Arsenal's goalscoring record. The reward was participation in a presentation at a school assembly that we were told he would attend. When the assembly bottomed out, he sent a fax through, and I was invited into a staff room to take a phone call with his agent.

Or when he turned out at a community day event in Catford, him standing and making small talk with my parents, my brother and me tangled at their knees, watching the boy from the neighbourhood speak with the West African immigrants who had made the neighbourhood their new home.

//

The bonds between South London's professional football clubs and the region's young kids begins early. Saturday morning training sessions became rumours of a football team on Hilly Fields. We cast ballots to pick the name. I wrote 'Hilly Rangers' on some paper. My brother wrote something similar. Neither of us was picked. The club was officially registered, and in 1999 Hillyfielders FC was born.

We played our home games on the rec in deep green kits and still trained on Saturday mornings. Volunteer coaches managed the teams. Some weekends Crystal Palace would gift the club tickets, and so I attended my first football match proper in that period, a league game at Selhurst Park. A band of Hillyfielders FC families convoyed out of Lewisham and down through Sydenham and Forest Hill, a borough-to-borough road trip with boys I have long forgotten. We sat in the family stand, waved claret-and-blue scarfs and felt ancient Palace chants swell in our thin throats, then went home and tried to spot ourselves on the telly.

For as long as I can recollect, South London's three major footballing institutions – Crystal Palace, Charlton and Millwall – have retained strong relations with the communities who sustain them, have spread long arms into local areas and pulled new talent from the earth, mining the ground for Black gold.

The Crystal Palace youth system has become a staple in South London, an academy famed for turning out a staggering line of 'touchline' Black footballers – wingers and full-backs who have come to dominate the tight spaces of football league flanks. Wilfried Zaha and Nathaniel Clyne, Wayne Routledge and Victor Moses are among that expanding dynasty.

At my second primary school in Bromley, where we moved in 2001, a community coach from the club delivered after-school sessions for kids interested in football. After impressing, my brother was invited to trial at Crystal Palace, and so one evening a week we would travel with my father to the Palace training ground in Beckenham, see the famed evergreen hedges crowding the training pitches, the chairman walking through the car park, professional footballers disappearing into the darkness, a sharp enthusiasm rising among us, the belief that maybe this here was the real deal.

'We are a South London club and it is important we had a training ground close to our stadium,' said Stephen Browett, former Palace co-chairman, to a local paper in 2013.[3] 'If we didn't have Beckenham and moved to a training ground further out somewhere, it would make it difficult for kids from Croydon, Lambeth, Southwark, Wandsworth and Bromley to come.'

Nothing ever came of those trials, but my brother and I still speak about the sessions, tease about how we were young kids who could've gone pro *if not but*. We reshape our memories to include encounters with the players who eventually made the grade, those who would gain pro contracts and those we still see something of ourselves in.

At the turn of every generation, South London presents an icon, a player who comes to mean more, whose brilliance on the pitch and whose identity away from it shifts his relationship with those who stand and support from the sidelines. Ian Wright *179 Just Done It* gave way to Rio Ferdinand, with his deep ties to Peckham and his crowning as one of the finest central defenders in British history. When Ferdinand left the game, the mantle was thrust onto Wilfried Zaha.

Zaha arrived at a time when a generation of Black footballers from South London were passing guard to the next, prolific league careers cantering towards their twilight. I watched Lambeth-born midfielder Jason Euell at pre-season games at Charlton before he ended things at AFC Wimbledon. I saw the centre-back Sam Sodje, a Nigerian international, in a Charlton team that travelled to the south coast and defeated

Wilfried Zaha takes flight in an early game for Crystal Palace. He made his first-team debut in 2010.

Southampton on a bitter November afternoon. He retired at Portsmouth in 2013.

I heard the rumours of Anton Ferdinand sitting in my barber shop on Lee High Road, his signed West Ham poster hanging over the men trimming knotted afros into skin fades through the afternoons and the early evenings. They were local icons glimpsed from afar, fruits of the South London soil living in six degrees of separation, their careers backing out into the darkness, ready for a new clutch of kids from the same regions to emerge.

Among the first of Zaha's generation to surface was the midfield prodigy John Bostock. His name floated through secondary schools, whispers on the wind from friends who still played at Palace on weekday evenings, arriving to school the next day with tales about the grace they had seen. He was an anomaly, a marvel of his time of whom greatness was expected, signed by Palace at five years old and playing for the first team at fifteen.

After Bostock's premature emergence, the remainder of our generation followed. In 2010, when Crystal Palace had been bought by a group of fans known as CPFC 2010, the club tabled a new strategy to place the club at the core of their local community. They erected billboards across the region with a slogan that read 'South London and Proud', the mantra flying alongside images of the club's local stars of tomorrow. Zaha was among the academy squad members selected to appear in the campaign.

Zaha was born in Abidjan, Côte d'Ivoire and was raised in Thornton Heath, in a house so close to Selhurst Park that he remembers seeing the floodlights shimmering from the stands as a young boy. He played his first football for local Croydon team Whitehorse Wanderers and has been intertwined with Crystal Palace since he was scouted aged eight. His presence in the Premier League, and his relationship with the country at large, have begun to throw light on the nuances of identity and home for Black British people, for the generations of African and Caribbean families raised in the old traditions of a new country. In that passing of time, they have slowly been carving out an identity of their own.

Zaha was an England international until the age of twenty. He played for the under-19s and the under-21s and for the full team at Wembley. Many of his friends who he grew with through the youth systems still turn out for the national team today. But in 2016, three years after his last performance (a friendly against Scotland), Zaha pledged international allegiance to his birth country, Côte d'Ivoire. In response, England manager Gareth Southgate said:

> If you don't feel that internal 100 per cent passion for England, then I'm not sure it's for me to sell that to you. It should be your desire to do it. Although I'm always willing to sit down with players, it should be them coming to us ... the inherent desire of wanting to play for your country is the most important thing.[4]

Southgate's comments hinted at a subtle misunderstanding of kids with dual heritages, an inability to recognise the shifting sense of home that can exist for those like Zaha, for those like me. For many first- and second-generation immigrants whose parents or grandparents found new homes in Britain, whose recent family lines are staggered across the continents, 'the inherent desire of wanting to play for your country' can manifest uneasily amid these tensions. Our passions are divided, our identities frayed. Our upbringings were British. Our families come from countries far from here. We carry their stories in our surnames. The matter of nationality is a complex one.

In that uneasy straddling of home countries and birthplaces, South London has become more than a region for some, an identity in itself, a holding space to balance the fragments of themselves that never quite fit, a piece of the land they cling to as distinctly their own. 'I just came here from the age of four and South London is all I know really,' Zaha said in an interview once,[5] years deep in the Premier League but still deeply local in his presence, still turning out at five-a-side pitches with friends in the summer, still driving his car over the same streets he rode his bike on to the stadium.

Among Zaha's generation of players who emerged from the Crystal Palace youth system, there are a scatter of Black boys bred in South London who wear varying international crests on their jerseys. Victor Moses played in the England youth system like Zaha and then turned out for Nigeria. Sean Scannell, of Jamaican heritage, who also featured on the billboard, pledged for Ireland, Nathaniel Clyne for England. John Bostock declared for Trinidad & Tobago. Dual heritage is encoded in South London's DNA. These footballers are emblems of these communities settled, the rising total of African countries they represent an indication of how the Black presence in South London has broadened between my generation and the first.

In 2013, when still playing for England, Zaha was asked about his Ivorian roots and his subsequent life in Britain. 'I think of myself as a Londoner more than anything else,' he said.[6]

//

The starry-eyed gaze we set upon footballers in our infancy begins to fade in our late twenties. John Bostock is twenty-nine now and plays his football for Doncaster Rovers in League One – a triumph in its own unique way. We never realised back then that, among many things, the kind of success you dream of in football is not a consequence of skill alone, but of mentality and divine timing. Of proper guidance and luck randomly allotted. After offers from Barcelona and a move to Tottenham at sixteen, he drifted quietly through the leagues across Europe – a season in Turkey, three more in Belgium – his story a footnote in South London folklore, another boy who, for a brief moment, flew close to the sun. The lower leagues are fuelled by these stories: Black footballers who never quite made the grade at the most elite level and now play their football in the national and regional leagues, boys I schooled with or had heard of who now turn out for Bromley and Cray Wanderers and Welling United.

Footballers are no longer our superheroes now, just men and women feeling their way through life the best way they know how. And so that fleeting sense of boyish wonder is inherited by the next generation, young cousins and family friends of mine being dragged gradually into ritual. As I moved through my twenties, I began to hear the similar stories, the chance encounters and rumours bonding them to local heroes: Rio Ferdinand saw a family friend of ours running late for school on a cold morning, stopped his car and drove him to the school gates; Rio Ferdinand spotted in a pie & mash shop on a local high street; the Wright-Phillips brothers Shaun and Bradley driving past my godbrother's old house in Crofton Park.

Tradition reaffirming itself for the young. Fingerprints of the past in their DNA.

I tore my hamstring when I was twenty-four. In the second half of a national cup game, I chased a breaking winger down a hard mud flank and felt the muscle shred behind the knee. I collapsed on the bobbled pitch, suffered a grade two tear, walked with crutches for weeks. My season was abruptly curbed. I broke with my Saturday routine for the first time since I was eleven.

Weekends that for so long had meant crumbling dressing rooms and faded kits at random sports grounds across South London and North Kent were now open. I filled the void with spare Charlton tickets from a friend and sat in the East Stand at The Valley for four, five, six games. Travelled away to Watford and to Millwall. Caught the team when they were quietly excited about a new generation of local players making their

Jason Euell playing for Charlton in 2001. After retiring in 2014, he returned to the club as an Academy and under-23s coach. In 2021, he was promoted to first-team coach.

way into the first team: Ademola Lookman, raised in Peckham by Nigerian immigrants, and Joe Gomez from Catford, son of a Gambian father and an English mother, both coached through Charlton's youth systems in part by Jason Euell (who has since been promoted to the role of first-team coach).

They are now part of a golden South London generation that in the years following my brief stay on the East Stand has gathered mass adulation across the British media, the subject of intense documentaries and broadsheet news spreads, a generation that has drawn comparisons with the French boys from the banlieues who won the country the World Cup in 2018 and the kids from the Catalan region who steered the Spanish national team to victory in two European Championships and a World Cup between 2008 and 2012.

With Jadon Sancho and Reiss Nelson, who grew up together on the Aylesbury Estate, not far from where Ryan Bertrand followed Rio Ferdinand out of the Friary Estate in Peckham, with Aaron Wan-Bissaka following a long line of Crystal Palace 'touchline' players, with Callum Hudson-Odoi and Jonathan Panzo, with the Sessegnon siblings and the Chalobah brothers, the rest of the country have come wise to a footballing legacy that has been at work for five decades. And with a World Cup on the horizon, they wait on in hope.

Hillyfielders FC still stands. The club is twenty-two years old. They moved grounds a few years back, down Brockley Road to Honor Oak Park, and now field fourteen teams across local leagues. Arsenal striker Eddie Nketiah had his start with the club, some forty years after Ian Wright charged up and down on the old home ground. Like many boys from across South London, Nketiah idolised Wright as a child. The two are friends now. When, aged twenty, Nketiah joined Leeds on loan in 2019, Wright would check in with him, offer advice and travel to Elland Road and watch him play.

'Growing up in similar areas, we can relate to each other,' Nketiah explained in an interview around the time. 'He was always open with me, giving me certain little tips and help.'[7] In another he said of Wright, 'Whenever I need to speak to somebody, he's always there and available.'[8] That sense of subtle affiliation to them both has led me to keep track of his career, and now whenever the name 'Nketiah' flashes across the screen I'm instinctively drawn to memories of the gaping greens and Saturday sessions on Hilly Fields. I dig out my laminated Hillyfielders membership card that still hangs in my mum's kitchen and reads 'Member 008', and wrestle with the thoughts that he and the club share the same birth year: 1999.

I think about how Nketiah, like so many others, is the sum of community parts: coaches and part-time staff, immigrant parents and professional footballers, pulling and turning in South London for generations, paving the road Eddie would walk from Lewisham to the Premier League.

I do not watch Nketiah how I watched Bostock or Scannell or Zaha, don't demand or expect a Premier League legend from his playing career. I know that his time in the game will be determined by the same weathering forces that met those who came before him, conditions of luck and divine timing and good guidance. But he has started well. He is the England under-21s all-time record goalscorer (edging out Alan Shearer and Francis Jeffers), with fourteen goals to his name.

A few weeks before Nketiah claimed the record, the Ghanaian national team manager C K Akonnor told a local radio station that the Ghanaian football association had reached out to Eddie's parents in an attempt to tease his national team loyalties back towards home. When asked about his Ghanaian heritage, Nketiah said, 'I'm very proud, it's in me, it's who I am and it's helped me to be the person I am today.'[9] The matter of nationality remains complex.

Nketiah is still in touch with his old club, and sends back videos at the start of every season wishing the kids good luck for the games ahead. For many, it will likely be their first encounters with a professional footballer, like mine with Ian Wright, like my family friends with Rio Ferdinand. And so, for a new generation, the cycle begins anew.

I can trace the lines now, join the dots between what happens out there on the giant stadium stages of the Premier League and the plastic posts fastened into grass playing fields in South London, realise that those early Saturday mornings on the rec were always about more than ourselves, more than what was, more than we could see, that the greater was somehow at work.

By many hands, a man is forged. The lone hero is a myth. We are all threads of something or someone else.

RAHEEM STERLING

A Portrait in Absence

Calum Jacobs

Historically, entering the world of professional sports was a profoundly political endeavor for black men. If you wanted to enter that world you had to be willing to push against racial boundaries and there was no real way to escape the political . . . professional sports was a location where many black males received their first education for critical consciousness about the politics of race .

bell hooks

***

listen children
keep this in the place
you have for keeping
always
keep it all ways

we have never hated black

listen
we have been ashamed
hopeless tired mad
but always

all ways
we loved us

we have always loved each other
children all ways

pass it on
Lucille Clifton

1

It's often remarked that footballers die twice – once when they retire and again when they actually pass. The same can also be said of their birth: players are born first into *the* world, and then they come into *our* world.

Avid football fans tend to become aware of talented young players long before they make their first-team debuts, via YouTube compilations set to EDM, youth tournaments, or the short clips that proliferate on football Twitter. These fans scrutinise the players' games closely, analysing these young footballers *as footballers*. Conversely, for more casual watchers footballers tend to come to their attention via the classist and racist narratives propagated by the right-wing mainstream media. This latter lens, by far the more culturally dominant, delineates a now-familiar cycle of emergence, vilification, and re-vilification of rising Black players by the press. Inevitably, it was via this route that Raheem Sterling entered into the wider footballing consciousness, the latest and largest avatar for a longstanding paradigm of denigration.

As important as it is to call out the malicious journalism and editorial choices that are at the heart of this process, to

Raheem Sterling poses for a portrait while with the England under-17 squad in 2011, one year before he announced himself to the British public by making his debut for Liverpool.

argue that they are the foundation of the problem is to ignore the enduring truths of history. Centuries before the nation knew Sterling's shape and form, the seeds of disinclination towards him had already been sown by England's colonial and imperialist past.

Speaking at the Du Bois Lectures at Harvard University in 1994, Jamaican-born cultural theorist and public intellectual Stuart Hall began with the following statement:

> When Europeans of the Old World first encountered the peoples and cultures of the New World in the 1400s, they put to themselves a great question: not 'Are you not a son and a brother, are you not a daughter and a sister?' ... but rather: 'Are these true men? Do they belong to the same species as us? Or are they born of another creation?'[1]

Presumably, what Hall posited was that any examination of the relationship between peoples who became the racialised 'other' and Western societies – and, in particular, the institutions those societies birthed – must be grounded in a foundational truth: that those who discovered new worlds justified their subsequent plunder and enslavement through the exclusion of people from the category 'human'. Historically, Black people, more than any other group, have been shut out of humanity. This fundamental debarring provided the foundational logic for the systemic dehumanisation – both overt and subtle – of Black people from that point onwards, flowing through the genesis of the transatlantic slave trade, the inception of the 'civilising' mission of colonialism and the so-called Enlightenment.

To this day, the legacy of the classification of Black people as something less than or other than human shapes political policy and much media engagement with Blackness. For any effort to unpack the relationship between Black public figures, the press, and the wider cultural apparatus that often comes to encircle and condemn them, it is crucial to keep this context at the fore.

Given the high levels of Black participation in football, it is no surprise that the game is one of the chief sites where this historically rooted hatred manifests most blatantly. The experience of Raheem Sterling, his takedown and subsequent redemptive arc – a warped fiction that reflects the amorality of the English media – is mapped so clearly that it can be witnessed from space. First, he was dragged before white Britain, degraded for non-existent infractions: the consumption of a Greggs pasty, the boarding of an EasyJet flight. Sterling's every off-pitch move was scrutinised and read as cultural transgression, his very existence presented as an affront to the moral sensibility of the country. Then, having weathered this treatment for years, keeping his counsel as he became a key cog in one of the Premier League's finest ever sides, in a 2018 Instagram post, Sterling held a mirror up to the tabloid media's racist double standards by juxtaposing two stories (one that disparagingly detailed Tosin Adarabioyo buying his mother a house and another that praised Phil Foden for doing the exact same thing) to demonstrate that this racist coverage was institutionalised. With the *Daily Mail* and *The Sun* temporarily backed into a defensive corner, the wider football industry began a prolonged self-analytical reckoning.

Sterling's efforts singlehandedly ushered in a new era of Black player power in Britain. His decision to push back against those who'd sought to destroy him – a choice that could have gone either way – not only ensured that no other Black player would be subject to the same degree of racist treatment, but engendered in those same players an inner belief in their ability to affect meaningful change.

Although Raheem Sterling was unavailable to lend his voice to this essay, given all that he has come to represent in British society – possession of the England captaincy in the absence of Harry Kane and Jordan Henderson alongside the award of an MBE in 2021 stand as testament to this – it would have been remiss of me not to include him in this book. Through this piece of writing we'll attempt to understand Sterling through a distinctly Black lens, specifically by seeking to understand his affinity with Jamaica. It's important to acknowledge that this framing won't create a more 'real' version of Sterling – only he can reveal that – but it will, based on the documents and knowledge available, attempt to pull together a more nuanced portrait of him.

2

White society constructs, holds and disseminates multiple often-contradictory notions of Blackness in its shared consciousness, a collective force that effectively pervades British culture. For example, the spurious 'danger' and 'darkness' baked into Blackness simultaneously incite the allure of the 'forbidden', as variously exemplified by the appropriation of Black cool, fetishisation, and enduring myths about hypersexuality. Although bewildering, this contradiction is culturally ubiquitous and widely understood (if not explicitly acknowledged). Equally common, but perhaps less well mapped, is the notion that Black people are ennobled by their 'struggle', and therefore capable of exerting a moralising force. On a day-to-day level, this takes the form of Black people functioning as educators within their social groups or places of work. It is also exemplified by 'diversity' programmes and panels, whereby white-dominated corporations and their white employees see themselves as engaged, active participants in 'the work', instructed by their Black moralisers.* Meanwhile, in the political sphere, particularly in

* Speaking at the University of Southern California's Bovard Auditorium in 2015, Angela Davis said: 'Diversity is a corporate strategy. It's a strategy designed to ensure that the institution functions in the same way that it functioned before, except that you now have some Black faces and brown faces. It's a difference that doesn't make a difference.'

the USA, Black voters – and particularly Black women – are time and again tasked with deposing right-wing candidates.

Scaled up, this concept is apparent in the retrospective hagiography of Black radical voices who were imprisoned or assassinated, such as Nelson Mandela and Martin Luther King Jr. At the time of his death, Martin Luther King Jr. was detested by white America for his 'unpatriotic' denouncement of the Vietnam War and bold political and socioeconomic agenda designed to forge alliance between poor Blacks and whites. Today, his direct action and incisive, scathing structural critiques have been abstracted by the establishment almost to the point of meaningless, a process novelist Namwali Serpell described as 'the grotesque Hallmarkification of one speech about dreams'.[2] In death, MLK functions as an apolitical moral authority, his radical legacy reductively manipulated and appropriated to rally for peace and love in the absence of justice.

Similarly, the popular contemporary conception is that Nelson Mandela was, to quote journalist Adam Roberts, 'an icon of peace and reconciliation; a symbol of forgiveness ... widely adored as a sort of Father Christmas character, chuckling into old age, patting small children on the head'.[3] Although it is true that Mandela's twenty-seven-year incarceration slowly transformed him into a mythic figure and an inspiration for Black South Africans, the Archbishop Desmond Tutu, another icon of the struggle against apartheid, once claimed that it would be misleading to think of Mandela as a saint. Madiba was formerly the head of the military wing of the African National Congress, which was formed in response to the brutality of the Sharpeville Massacre,* and therefore (justifiably) willing to use

* In the Black township of Sharpeville on 21 March, 1960, the South African police opened fire with submachine guns on unarmed anti-apartheid protesters, killing 69 men, women, and children, and wounding 180 more.

violence to advance its aims. Yet in the popular cultural imaginary, Mandela is diluted to a saintly figure, one far removed from the realities of his political leadership and pragmatic acceptance of the potential need for violence.

This narrative pattern of demonising a Black public figure before enveloping them in a mantle of near-hero worship while calling on them to 'solve' racism strips the individual of complexity, thereby reducing them to a commoditised emblem. It allows white society to abrogate the responsibility to tackle racism that they have run from for centuries by outsourcing the work of anti-racism to the magical Black figure. In the case of Raheem Sterling, this process can be witnessed in real time.

In an article for *The Sunday Times*, Alastair Campbell perfectly illustrated the concept, albeit accidentally.[4] The piece, titled 'How it feels to ... talk to Raheem Sterling about racist abuse', is a gushing summary of an interview Campbell conducted with the footballer for *GQ*. Describing Sterling as his 'new hero', Campbell opens by detailing the level of excitement that meeting Sterling fostered:

> 62-year-old men who have rubbed shoulders with kings and queens, presidents and prime ministers – and played in a charity football match with Diego Maradona – really shouldn't get excited about meeting 24-year-old footballers. But Raheem Sterling has recently, and rapidly, become one of those 'more than a sportsman' sportsmen.

To suggest that Sterling's impact extends beyond the football pitch is justified, but Campbell's assertion entirely overlooks the forty-year history of Black footballing forebears who suffered similar indignities, and who were also forced to be 'more than a sportsman'. Campbell also neglects to explain why he, as someone who held a key position of power in the British Government for several years, has done decidedly less anti-racism work than a young footballer. Rather than undertaking any self-reflection, Campbell, like most other liberal white men, is content to instead frame Sterling in the same saintly light as Mandela and King. He even tangentially invokes the late South African leader:

> The day before I interviewed him for *GQ*, the BBC football podcast was debating the question: 'Is Raheem Sterling the most influential sportsman in Britain?' When I told him it was like listening to a debate about Nelson Mandela … his smile was one more of bafflement than pride.

Despite what Campbell or anyone else proclaims, Raheem Sterling is not Nelson Mandela, and he is not Martin Luther King Jr. Neither should he be reductively compared to them purely by virtue of a willingness to vocalise his views on racism. However, it is not incidental that these are the two men he is likened to. Ossified in the pages of history, King and Mandela are divorced from their radicalism. The anodyne popularised versions of them that circulate do not threaten or discomfort whiteness or its grip on structural power – rather, they comfort it. The parallels with the cultural reaction to Sterling are marked.

Sterling's request that British newspaper editors 'have a second thought about fair publicity' was not accusatory. He did not use incendiary language and he did not make it about him. Brave as it was to speak out, his balanced framing tempered his point, making it more palatable, harder to contest and easier to commodify. Whereas Mandela and King's legacies were rewritten, the current system's stranglehold dictated that Sterling do that work for himself. That is not to discredit Sterling or his efforts. Rather, it should be considered evidence of a system that actively discourages radicalism and repackages hard-hitting perspectives in such a way to limit their scope to precipitate difficult feelings in white people or initiate material changes to the existing status quo. The danger inherent in this practice is discussed by Ben Carrington in his foundational text *Race, Sport and Politics*:

> The black athletic body (male and female) has become a powerful signifier within contemporary media culture. This signifier has increasingly served to redefine and in some sense reduce the agency of embodied freedom into a narrow set of 'power' and 'performance' motifs that are radically decontextualized from broader political movements, thus separating the black body from any connection to social change and hence to a depoliticization of the black athlete itself.[5]

Sterling is irrefutably part of football's anti-racism discourse, but it is important to question how he and others – either previously or contemporarily – came to occupy this position. Did he – does he – want to be football's anti-racism ambassador? Is it reasonable to festoon Sterling with this responsibility? Has he been press-ganged into the role by a society that continues to delegate anti-racism work to those who experience the consequences of it? Whatever Sterling's thoughts on how he became a spokesperson for anti-racism, he told *The Sunday Times* that he is no longer interested in being defined solely in this way: 'One of the things I'm probably trying to step away from now is I don't want to be seen as this figure for this reason or that reason.'[6]

Sterling's attempt to reposition himself should come as no surprise. Before his tragic passing, recency bias meant that Cyrille Regis was thought of solely as a retired footballer by younger fans. But when the Sisyphean task of confronting the racism that courses through football was bestowed upon him, he was as fresh-faced and youthful as Sterling is now, with no special attributes that would help him to magically withstand racial abuse. In his book *Pitch Black*, Emy Onuora expands on how unfair and daunting this task must have been:

> These ordinary black men from ordinary black communities instantly became role models, pioneers, ambassadors and the focal point for debates around national identity, just at the point at which they got their first foothold in the professional game. Most, if not all, of these players were ill prepared for the responsibility associated with their new found status as professional footballers, let alone as role models and pioneers.[7]

Sterling has so far worn this responsibility lightly – he does not seem to feel burdened by it. If anything, it appears to have matured him further, and helped him to understand the power he has to create opportunity and positive change through his charitable foundation. But ultimately his established public persona tells us little about the 'real' Raheem Sterling. And although his legacy is now inextricably linked to the fight against racism in football, given the fact that he has publicly stated that he no longer wishes to take the lead in tackling the issue, the time has clearly come for both Black and white Britons to understand him beyond the limiting scope of this role.

3

The histories of Jamaica and Britain are so entwined that any attempt to understand the countries as separate entities would be not just naive, but disingenuous. As Kehinde Andrews puts it in *Back to Black*, his unflinching reassessment of Black radical politics, 'The entire colony was designed, built and run to enrich Britain.'[8] The scale of this murderous operation was lucidly clarified by historian and educator Courtney Hay in the formerly banned 1978 documentary *Blacks Britannica*. Hay argued that Jamaica's ultimate contribution to Great Britain was the genesis of primitive accumulation that drove the industrial revolution:

> At one point, Britain was making four times as much profit out of one Caribbean island [Jamaica], which is sugar production, as it did out of all its trade with the rest of the world. So that was the level of profit that Black people were generating into Britain.[9]

The irrefutable truth is that even before the Empire 'came home' in 1948 and the census began to reflect the number of Jamaicans who would dramatically reshape the cultural and political terrain of Great Britain, Jamaica's economic impact had been tremendous. But when it comes to the matter of what Jamaicans represent in the imagination of the wider (white) British consciousness, historical analyses have tended to centre on the all-too-familiar notion of Jamaicans as an unwelcome surge of unruly 'outsiders' – a label readily applied to all non-white citizens of the Commonwealth who paid to, and lived a life in service of, their 'mother country'.

Considerable emphasis has been placed on examining why white Britons behave how they do, despite the deep historical relationship between their country and Jamaica, and the fact that Jamaican people produced the sugar that paid for much of Great Britain's architecture. However, attempts to understand the irrationality of white hostility once again place the perception and experiences of white people at the centre, and serve as yet another reminder of the unjust nature of things, which Black people are so instinctively familiar with – a forced ingestion of the trauma that Black people already know and feel so well. Wider efforts to combat this predictable white attitude have included actively celebrating the contribution that immigrants have made to this nation. But we should ask ourselves: who does this serve? After all, Black people need no reminders of their self-evident ability to enrich the nation, while the white general population prove – most overtly through the political parties and policies that they vote for – that they are ultimately unmoved by these celebrations. It would be more powerful to unpack and celebrate the rich and real connections British-Jamaicans share with their homelands, and how this cross-continental bridge building defines and fortifies their sense of self.

Although Sterling left Jamaica at the age of five to join his mother in England, he can still recall his early years in Kingston so vividly you'd think he left last week. It's in these moments that the guardedness and mild defensiveness of his media training fall away, as youthful enthusiasm fills his features and enlivens his spirit. Speaking to *The Players' Tribune* in October 2020, Sterling described with clarity the pure pleasure of rushing outside into balmy tropical cloudbursts, splashing in puddles and showering in rainfall, as well as the frequency with which he begged his grandmother for money to buy Grape-Nuts ice creams from a local convenience store, where almost any household item could be procured. 'This guy used to run a little shop out of his house,' he recalled. 'So you'd run over after playing football all day in the street and you'd knock on the door and then, literally, his head would just pop out this little window, like, "Oi, wha' you need?"'

The shop and its owner, whom Sterling describes as typifying the innate hustling spirit found in all Jamaicans, will be immediately recognisable to anyone with ancestral ties to the wider Caribbean. In these brief, colourful vignettes, Sterling is in communion with his Black audience and his home. In searching for explanations as to why a boy raised mostly in the sprawling grey landscape of West London remains so wedded to his Jamaican identity – like so many other Jamaican Brits – one might reference the obdurate antagonism of white Britain, or perhaps a deeply rooted incompatibility with the country's social mores. After all, as the great C L R James said, Caribbean migrants to the UK are 'in but not of Europe'.

While these interpretations ring true, to wholly endorse them would risk stripping members of the African diaspora of agency by confining their behaviour to the restrictive dynamic of oppression and resistance. Black people are not known to themselves and others purely through the forces of white supremacy. There is a deeper, far more communally grounded animus than that. Taking immigrant ethnic enclaves as a rich and illustrative example, it is possible to put forward a history that exists outside the strictures of subjugation and resistance, one that not only acknowledges but also celebrates diasporic agency.

Often derided by dominant white societies as 'evidence' of an inability to integrate, ethnic enclaves offer countless fundamental benefits to the immigrant communities that create and shape them – including economic security, the chance of social mobility, and communal identification that they can find nowhere else.

While years of prolonged gentrification have massively displaced Brixton's Black community, it once stood as the definitive Afro-Caribbean ethnic enclave that teemed with stores selling hard dough bread, salt fish and sugar cane, where the streets moved with rhythm and poetry. The area – which housed the first waves of Jamaican immigrants who arrived on the HMT *Empire Windrush* – hummed with a vibrancy that Jamaican residents recognised as something approximating their birthplaces. Its importance to Jamaican immigrants is reflected both in Donald Hinds's reflective 1966 part-memoir *Journey to an Illusion*,[10] in which he interviews fellow Jamaican immigrants about their experiences of settling in England, and in Colin Grant's 2019 book *Homecoming*.[11]

Sterling has spoken openly of moving between residences as his mother dealt with fluctuating rents – often receiving texts of new addresses as he made his way home – but he was not raised in Brixton. Instead he grew up in Neasden, an area that, while it may lack Brixton's rich cultural history of Afro-Caribbean community, is not without ties to Sterling's heritage and could feasibly have functioned as an ethnic enclave. Before Sterling's family settled on St Raphael's Estate (where George the Poet also grew up), it was already home to many Afro-Caribbean families. While we can't know for certain if this influenced Nadine Sterling to make Neasden their home, it wouldn't be a stretch to presume that an awareness of the presence of other Jamaican families on the estate eased the family's transition to their new environment. Tangentially, but not incidentally, Trojan Records, a label famed for introducing Jamaican music to a global audience, was also based in the area, having been founded in 1968 on Neasden Lane. It is therefore possible to speculate that Sterling's Jamaican heritage was fully entwined in his new life in Britain.

Ethnic enclaves are also naturally formed in the home. They allow families to freely practise the cultural patterns that form and shape their interior lives – whether that be speaking in patois, cooking stew chicken and rice, or simply expressing themselves freely without fear or judgement – and help to ensure that bonds with their ancestry are never broken. Baroness Floella Benjamin touched on the wider function of the Black home on *Desert Island Discs* in October 2020.[12] Although her family's initial, prospective visit to what would become their home in Beckenham was marred by their soon-to-be white neighbours calling the police to investigate their presence – an experience familiar to all Black people, irrespective of background* – Benjamin brought her characteristically uplifting tone to her recollections. When asked how she was able to effectively make light of the myriad forms of racial abuse she and her family endured, Benjamin replied:

> We had joy in our homes. It was joyful. Joyful within your home existence. You knew when you left your wonderful environment, your loving environment, and you stepped out the front door, you knew you were going to have to face whatever abuse came at you. But if you're prepared [by your home] for whatever comes in life, then you can cope with it.

* On 16 June 2009, Harvard professor Henry Louis Gates was arrested inside his Cambridge, MA home by a local police officer after his (white) neighbours witnessed him forcing open his own front door. Despite producing evidence that he was inside his own home, he was still taken into custody. On 14 February 2017 Metropolitan Police officers kicked down the front door of British rapper Stormzy's home. Scotland Yard said they were responding to a report of conspiracy to burgle and had thought that the flat was empty. Meanwhile, in an appearance on the *Longform* podcast in September 2020, the award-winning poet and essayist Claudia Rankine revealed that, while attending to the security system in her own home, police officers arrived and would not leave until her white husband assured them that she lived there.

This specific idea of emotional resilience being built through the joy found in familial love and the broader comfort and safety of the Black home has been explored by bell hooks:

> We have to see our homes as places of resistance. We have to look at our history and how much was started in the home. How much activism – Mary McLeod Bethune starting Bethune-Cookman College in her living room ... Why is our gaze so turned toward the master and mistress that we can't turn it toward ourselves and say: 'I believe that my home is the one place that I can make myself affirmed.' I tell people when I walk in my house it's like two arms jump out and hold me and say, 'Baby you are here. This is where you belong.'[13]

Sterling's astounding capacity to weather both the explicit and subtler forms of vitriol doled out by the right-wing media and endemic in white society can be traced to this same origin. His mental fortitude – a prerequisite for all footballers but arguably doubly for Black footballers – was integral to this resilience, but perhaps even more important was a home environment heavily influenced by Jamaican cultural norms. That experience afforded him an emotional and psychological refuge from the outside world, a buffer against the racialised hatred directed at him.

In a 2020 interview, Raheem confirmed that his home functioned as a cultural enclave defined by tough love that many British Jamaican children will recognise, but that also stands in stark contrast to the generally liberal attitudes of many white British parents towards child rearing. 'I grew up in London ... but at the same time it's a Jamaican household,' he said. 'There were a lot of rules in my house, which I think there are in a lot of [Jamaican] houses, but there were extra rules in my house ...

But then you grow up and you are very grateful. Tough love. A lot of tough love.'[14] In that same interview, he revealed that his mother Nadine exemplified hooks's ideas about the protective role of the Black home: 'There was always the thought of something could go wrong and you're safer in your house. Basically, what could be avoided, avoid it.'

Sterling now proudly lays claim to his heritage on social media – by preparing Jamaican food in his kitchen or displaying his friendships with Jamaican or British-Jamaican compatriots, including Jamaican international footballer Leon Bailey, Jamaican cricketer Chris Gayle and Usain Bolt.

The words of historian Dilip Hiro contextualises this newly displayed pride (which Sterling understandably concealed while various right-wing newspapers sought to demonise him) and its psychological benefits: 'The point about being proud of what one is, is so fundamental to normal human existence that it allows no compromise.'[15] Furthermore, Raheem practises a specific kind of affirming self-love, which more than likely came from his mother. 'My mum has taught me how to love myself, how to love my skin colour,' he told Campbell in that *GQ* interview. This preparation stemmed from an early recognition that he would need to do so because British society would not.

4

To build a rich understanding of Sterling's racial and cultural identity, a holistic reading is required. Unpacking material that details his position and perspective as rooted in Great Britain – where he built his life and career – is key, but only when he is contextualised through his Jamaican heritage does a more comprehensive portrait of the man emerge.

Britain often compels first- and second-generation members of the African diaspora to grapple with multiple anxieties of belonging. Whether Raheem feels the existential tension that this responsibility tends to generate we cannot know for sure. What is clear, however, is that since his purported moral resurrection, he has come to exist at the centre of an interconnected network of competing interests, each one vying for his attention and applying pressure: his parent club, the England national team and numerous brand 'tie-ups'.

However, the intensity of these commitments melts away under the sun in Jamaica – sliding off his back as gently as the waves of the Caribbean Sea lap the shores of Ocho Rios. Jamaica, Sterling said in an interview with *The Guardian*, is a place where 'time moves so slow'. 'When I go down there,' he revealed, 'I'm in paradise, beaches every day – just chilling,

Raheem Sterling's unconcealed pride in his Jamaican heritage is working to enlarge and enrich British-Jamaican identity.

literally chilling. That's why I have to go back: the beaches, the food. I love every moment of it.'[16]

'I actually feel emotional when I have to leave,' Sterling continued. 'Really emotional because ... because the food is just fresh, you sit on the beach and it's coming out from the sea – fresh, the fish is fresh. Oh please don't – please don't remind me!' The feelings that leaving Jamaica to return to England give rise to in Sterling parallel the stirring of melancholy that Stuart Hall describes in his memoir *Familiar Stranger* as he departs Jamaica:

> Whenever I am flying back to England after spending time in the Caribbean and look through the aircraft window at the island below slowly receding into the distance, I'm assailed by a wave of melancholia which always arises in me in relation to Jamaica as the lost object of desire.[17]

The contrasts in tempo and texture that emerge between the two islands, and their inhabitants – both of which Sterling and Hall know well – are marked. Of these differences, Hall wrote:

> I knew about the stereotypical British stiff upper lip. But what impressed me more immediately was the tensed way the English inhabited their bodies: a 'settledness-in-place', a visceral resistance to movement, to fluidity, to letting go. People in the Caribbean simply carry their bodies in a slacker way.[18]

Sterling, meanwhile, understands that his interactions with fellow Jamaicans reveal their essential character:

> They've got that straight face like they don't really want a picture but they do really ... Because obviously you're with a lot

> of your friends, and Jamaicans – sometimes they come across as aggressive, so I think they don't really want to approach to ask me there. But it's always a laugh. They are lovely people.[19]

The story of immigration feels largely singular. In both a real and philosophical sense, the migrant's journey is mined for evidence of what was lost in the transition, proof of the irreconcilability between the old and new reality is established and, finally, an enduring sense of incompleteness is rendered in the émigré, even as they work to forge a life in their new homeland. This narrative, which is streaked with the psychic and physical pain of displacement and discontent, is endlessly repeated, and remains our common conception of the process.

In proudly marrying – without contradiction – his pride in captaining the English national team to his aforementioned preference for spending time in his birth country, the cultural enclavism of his home and all the Jamaican idiosyncrasies that he expresses in public when he feels comfortable, Sterling gloriously challenges this established and widely accepted paradigm.

5

While it's true that many Jamaican members of the Windrush generation came to inhabit a state of temporariness – neither able to leave England nor to return to Jamaica as planned – for others, putting down roots and building lives felt like an achievement. Less is clearly understood about the attitudes and intentions of their descendants towards their Jamaican roots. I spoke with five British-Jamaican individuals to gain an understanding of how they relate to Jamaica, with the hope that their experiences would variously shade into and overlap with Raheem's. In this way, my intention was that their words would help us to build a richer, more detailed portrait of his emotions in relation to Jamaica.

Like Sterling, the people I spoke with have spent the bulk of their lives in Britain (in fact, all are second- or third-generation UK citizens). To retain a physical connection to Jamaica, each interviewee discussed their reliance on cultural enclaves and trips 'home' to their parents' and grandparents' birthplaces. However, this distance – both temporal and physical – doesn't inherently lessen the country's grip on their identities.

As Daniel McIntosh, a solicitor from North West London, explained:

> My Jamaican heritage has fundamentally shaped who I am as a person, how I view the world, and the way that I move and navigate within it. From the way that I speak – for example, my tone, inflections, and word structure – through to the way that I eat, to how I see the role of the family.

For writer and journalist Gena-mour Barrett, an annual trip to Jamaica to visit her grandmother reinforces her cultural identity: 'Ninety per cent of my family are Jamaican-born, so it's been a huge part of my identity. I'd say my grandparents have had the most influence on me culturally.' Author Candice Carty-Williams reiterated this position:

> Growing up and learning more about being Jamaican gave me something I knew a lot of my white peers didn't have. It's a culture, it's a way of living, and because Jamaica is so tiny and so influential, so much of the music, the ways of island living and proverbs have made their way over here. Now, as an adult, I classify myself as Jamaican-British (Jamaican first)

because, even though I don't live there, it's where I understand home is.

For lighting director Meshach Roberts, Jamaica's influence affected how he was perceived in Britain: 'It shaped how I was viewed – I was looked on to know reggae and dancehall by friends who weren't Jamaican.' Meshach's Scottish-Jamaican identity, formed in his home, but also in relation to a wider Jamaican community in London, is 'linked and layered, based on city and heritage', and has helped him to 'create a sense of self that is not just an antithesis to English identity'. According to Daniel, a careful distinction must be made between the Jamaican identity of those who are born and live on the island, and the British-Jamaican identity that exists in a specifically British context. 'There is British-Jamaican culture that has developed [here] over the last seventy years,' he told me, 'and that is not the same as my Jamaican heritage in general.'

While Sterling was born in Jamaica, by his own admission – his labelling of Jamaicans as 'they' rather than 'we' – when he returns, he's somewhat of an outlander. Setting aside his wealth, which insulates and affords him and his family a level of comfort and security, this realisation isn't necessarily a negative one. As Meshach explained it, although his 'clothes, stance and speech' indicate to locals that he isn't Jamaican-born, that doesn't lessen the sense of kinship felt: 'I think that it is appreciated that at surface level I am not [one of them] but in deeper ways I am connected, and that was a big realisation.' Daniel summed up the inherent complexity, and the contradictory emotions, engendered by 'coming' from a place you do not truly belong to, of being both and neither. 'I feel comfortable in my own skin in Jamaica,' he said. 'It doesn't feel like home, but it does feel familiar.'

Being in Jamaica has a similar effect on photographer Chad Mclean as it does on Sterling: 'My mum's from Manchester Parish, a place called Mandeville, the dirt is red and the trees are big and it's cooler, I think because of the altitude. It's just nice ... the mango trees ... family ... you forget about life and everything is just cool.' For Meshach, landing in Kingston and being hit by the heat and humidity in the air is an evocative signifier that he is back in the familiar embrace of the island:

> It was always dark by the time we were out of the airport, driving along the coastal road to where my family lives. We would have the smell of burning rubbish and bush, which was rich and not unpleasant, but just that heavy air of smoke and music whistling in used to let me know I was there.

Gena's experience of being led into the interior of the island on a journey to her grandmother's home gave her an appreciation of Jamaica's natural sublimity. 'We always stay at my grandparents' house, and to get there it's a long drive to "country", up and down winding roads atop cliffs surrounded by nature,' she said. 'I remember the year I was old enough to really understand how idyllic it actually was. It's like paradise.'

This sense of a precious connection, capable of reaching across generations while grounding, defining and comforting returnees shines through in Chad's description of the intangible things he treasures most when he returns to Mandeville. 'Hearing my grandad's indistinctive chatter brings me joy,' he began. 'I don't know what it is. It's like the challenge of piecing together what he's saying, like picking out the words that you understand from his low mumbling.' For Gena, this instinctual feeling is associated with the sight of her grandmother's tears as she greets her and her mother at the airport. 'She cries every single time we arrive,' she told me. 'I also think of my grandparents' pub next door to the house, named "Seymour", which is partly where my first name derives from.'

For Meshach, the day-to-day rhythm of life – 'going to a dance, sitting in a bar and just not doing a lot and also talking about nothing much to people' – are all he needs to feel content and at one with his surroundings. Candice, meanwhile, never feels more in touch with herself than when swimming in the Jamaican sea, or when clutching a bottle of Ting, a drink 'so inherently Jamaican', she told me, 'that I'm surprised it's even sold in the UK'. Daniel is mentally and physically comforted by the knowledge that, for the duration of his stay, he will have the sun on his skin on a daily basis. He also feels much more at ease in 'a predominantly Black environment'.

Each of their perspectives shines light on a particular nuance of the British-Jamaican experience, laying it bare for exploration. Unlike many of their forebears, none wish to return to Jamaica permanently. Instead, the country represents a temporary sanctuary, a nourishing retreat, and, in some cases, an aspirational second home. 'I'd prefer to split time between Britain and Jamaica,' Gena told me. 'I'd love to have a family vacation home, so when I return we could all stay there together ... I haven't given up on the dream yet.' In the very far future, Candice shared, 'I would love to be able to build a little house there by the sea, and go and spend three months of the year there. In winter, obviously.'

The capacity to simultaneously inhabit two seemingly disparate worlds, while feeling intimately connected to both – as Raheem does – is not a trait unique to the British-Jamaican experience. But the collective perception these British-Jamaicans have of Sterling is unambiguous. 'He's Jamaican through and through. Don't let anybody tell you any different,' said Chad.

'I would say that he is Jamaican,' Daniel agreed, but tempers this statement with an acknowledgement that it is assumptive. Meshach had no room for such equivocation: 'Sterling is Jamaican, no doubt.'

While their understanding of his nationality is ultimately irrelevant, it's telling that they recognise in Sterling subtle signals that have worked to build a cultural partition between him and them, despite the fact they've all spent the majority of their lives in England. It's clear that this conception is not meant to build distance; rather, it's rooted in a deep sense of pride. Like Bob Marley, Usain Bolt, Popcaan and other contemporary Jamaican cultural exports, Sterling allows British-Jamaicans the ability to point and exclaim: 'Nuh undaestimate wi, wi likkle but wi tallawah,' or 'We may be a small contingent in this country, but our impact relative to that is mighty.'

Sterling's ability to lay claim to his heritage without having his allegiance to England questioned marks a divergence from the recent past. Jimmy Greaves – in an article penned in the 1990s – attempted to exclude and undermine John Barnes on a similar basis.[20] 'Barnes was never a hero' wrote Paul Gilroy in the foreword to *'Race', Sport and British Society*.[21] He continued:

> Greavsie and company made his exclusion from the inner circle of British sporting greatness a matter of national honour ... he could never really be one of them/us while he retained a Jamaican passport ... A cat can be born in a kipper box but that, as we've been sagely told in a cynical echo of neo-fascist discourse, will never make it into a kipper.

The targeted terrorisation, detention, and illegal deportation of Jamaican-born British citizens is a reminder of just how fragile and contingent claims of belonging can be, and that attributing Sterling's ability to confidently embody two distinct cultures to a softening of attitudes towards British-Caribbean people in the UK is both naive and insensitive. However, even as the Conservative governments of Theresa May and Boris Johnson have used political levers to narrow the definition of Englishness with all the violence of a tightening noose, culturally (and socially) the country is moving inexorably in the opposite direction.

Whether consciously or not, Raheem Sterling has, as all immigrants must, amalgamated his ancestral history with his new life in a manner that has transformed him into a more complex individual, placing him at the forefront of much of this change. His unconcealed pride in his cultural heritage, which manifests on both a micro – his mannerisms, the inflections in his voice when he's relaxed – and macro – the creation of a shoe with Clarks, a brand so synonymous with Jamaica that many assume it originated there – level, work to develop and enrich British-Jamaican identity in ways that are immeasurably valuable and far-reaching. For that reason, they will be felt for generations to come.

Notes

INTRODUCTION

1 Smith, L T. (1999) *Decolonizing Methodologies: Research and Indigenous peoples*. New York: Palgrave, p193.

2 Back, L, Crabbe, T and Solomos, J. (1999) Beyond the racist/hooligan couplet: race, social theory and football culture. *British Journal of Sociology* 50(3) pp419–42, p425.

3 Back et al, p426.

4 Gilroy, P. (1993) *The Black Atlantic: Modernity and Double Consciousness*. London: Verso, p216.

5 Achebe, C. (2018) *Africa's Tarnished Name*. London: Penguin Random House, p33.

6 Onuora, E. (2015) *Pitch Black*. Hull: Biteback Publishing, p299.

7 Back L, et al, p430.

8 Sterling, R, Scott, A, Gray, A. (2020)

9 McLoughlin, D. (2021) Racial bias in football commentary (study): the pace and power effect. *Run Repeat*, 2 March. Available at https://runrepeat.com/racial-bias-study-soccer.

10 Brand, R. (2018) *Under The Skin* #059: Black revolution & whiteness psychosis (with Kehinde Andrews) [Podcast]. Available at https://www.stitcher.com/show/under-the-skin/episode/059-black-revolution-whiteness-psychosis-with-kehinde-andrews-57852129.

11 Jackson, L M. (2019) What's missing from *White Fragility*. *Slate*, 4 September. Available at https://slate.com/human-interest/2019/09/white-fragility-robin-diangelo-workshop.html.

12 Hughes, M. (2018) Racism would be far worse without football. *The Times*, 13 December. Available at https://www.thetimes.co.uk/edition/sport/racism-would-be-far-worse-without-football-zww7l23dx.

13 Carrington, B. (2010) *Race, Sport and Politics: the Sporting Black Diaspora*. London: SAGE Publications, p175.

14 Sharpe C. (2019) Still here. York University. Available at https://utpjournals.press/doi/pdf/10.3138/topia.2019-0013.

15 Morrisey, P. (2020) Club statement: taking the knee. 21 September. Available at https://www.qpr.co.uk/news/club-news/club-statement-taking-the-knee/.

16 Ramazzotti, A. (2019) Lukaku case, Thuram: 'Fermatevi o siete conniventi'. *Corriere dello Sport*, 4 September. Available at https://www.corrieredellosport.it/news/calcio/2019/09/04-60734756/caso_lukaku_thuram_fermatevi_o_siete_conniventi/.

17 Bryant, H. (2020) Why black athletes run from black identity. *The Undefeated*, 17 February. Available at https://theundefeated.com/features/why-black-athletes-run-from-black-identity/.

18 Ahmed, S. (2017) *Living a Feminist Life*. London: Duke University Press, p37.

19 Parker, R J. (2019) 'Black people work from the position of "we"': an interview with Carrie Mae Weems. *Frieze*, 25 October. Available at https://www.frieze.com/article/black-people-work-position-we-interview-carrie-mae-weems.

20 Sterling, R. (2019) Raheem Sterling: I don't want the next generation to suffer like me. *The Times*, 23 April. Available at https://www.thetimes.co.uk/article/raheem-sterling-i-dont-want-the-next-generation-to-suffer-like-me-5ng7tpqkq.

21 Macharia, K. (2018) black (beyond negation). *The New Inquiry*, 26 May. Available at https://thenewinquiry.com/blog/black-beyond-negation/.

TOMORROW NEVER CAME

1 *Forbidden Games* (2017) Directed by J Carey and A Darke. Available at: Netflix.

2 Joseph, C. (2019) 'I was a monster to Justin': 21 years after the death of his gay brother, John Fashanu opens up on regret of being part of the culture which condemned him to death and why he is now trying to help others come out. *Mail on Sunday*, 16 March. Available at https://www.dailymail.co.uk/sport/football/article-6817615/John-Fashanu-opens-regret-brother-Justins-death.html.

3 Murphy, S, et al. (2020) Race commission head Tony Sewell apologises for anti-gay comments. *The Guardian*, 16 July. Available at https://www.theguardian.com/world/2020/jul/16/concern-choice-charity-boss-tony-sewell-head-uk-race-commission.

LIFE AT THE VANGUARD, AGAIN AND AGAIN

1 BBC News. Entertainment, Parkinson shows Wright the red card. *BBC News*, 5 Jan. Available at http://news.bbc.co.uk/1/hi/entertainment/249010.stm.

2 Gilroy, P. (1993) *Small Acts: Thoughts on the Politics of Black Cultures*. London: Serpent's Tail, pp75–76.

I DID IT MY WAY

1 Perry, K. (2014) Britain and the politics of race in the 20th century. *History Compass* 12(8) pp651–63, p651.
2 *Pathé Reporter Meets Jamaicans Come to Britain to Look for Work* (1948) Produced by British Pathé. London: British Pathé.
3 Davison, R B. (1962) *West Indian Migrants: Social and Economic Facts of Migration From the West Indies*. London: Institute of Race Relations.
4 Hiro, D. (1971) *Black British, White British*. London: Eyre & Spottiswoode, p17.
5 Sadlier, R. (2020) Episode 1766: *The Player's Chair* with Andy Cole [Podcast]. Available at https://www.secondcaptains.com/2020/05/13/episode-1766-the-players-chair-with-andy-cole/.
6 Cole, A, Fenton, P. (1999) *Andy Cole: The Autobiography*. Manchester: Manchester United Books, p6.
7 *Windrush: A New Generation* (2001) BBC Four.
8 Gilroy, P. (2011) *Black Britain: A Photographic History*. London: Saqi Books, p119.
9 Cole, A, Fenton, P, p21.
10 Cole, A, Fenton, P, p23.
11 Cole, A, Fenton, P, p25.
12 Cole, A, Fenton, P, p27.
13 Wright, I. (2020) Welcome to *Wrighty's House* [Podcast]. Available at. https://www.theringer.com/2020/10/28/21537980/welcome-to-wrightys-house.
14 Cole, A, Fenton, P, p41.
15 Cole, A, Fenton, P, p61.
16 Cole, A, Fenton, P, p72.
17 Cole, A, Fenton, P, p127.
18 Cole, A, Fenton, P, p166.
19 Selvon, S. (2006) *The Lonely Londoners*. London: Penguin Classics, p126.
20 Onuora, E. (2015) *Pitch Black*. Hull: Biteback Publishing, p18.
21 Moor, N. (2010) The big interview: Andy Cole – 'Playing with Dwight Yorke was like meeting a special woman and falling in love'. *FourFourTwo*, 3 February. Available at https://www.fourfourtwo.

com/features/andy-cole-playing-yorke-was-meeting-a-special-woman-and-falling-love.

22 hooks, b (2004) *We Real Cool: Black Men and Masculinity*. London: Routledge, p143.

23 Harris, D. (2013) *The Promised Land: Manchester United's Historic Treble*. Edinburgh: Arena Sport, pp87–88.

24 Harris, D, pp87–88.

THE ACCIDENTAL TRAILBLAZER

1 Riley-Jones, A. (2020) Hope Powell on her life in football. *Great British Life*, 10 March. Available at https://www.greatbritishlife.co.uk/people/hope-powell-7273222.

2 Cadwalladr, C. (2011) Hope Powell: 'I was the real-life *Bend It Like Beckham* girl'. *The Guardian*, 12 June. Available at https://www.theguardian.com/football/2011/jun/12/women-football-hope-powell-interview.

3 Powell, H. (2016) *Hope: My Life in Football*. London: Bloomsbury Sport, pp42–43.

4 Powell, H, pp32–33.

5 Powell, H. (2017) The journey: being first. *The Coaches' Voice*. Available at https://www.coachesvoice.com/being-first/.

6 Naylor, A. (2020) 'I didn't go "Oh, I'm a black woman", I just thought "I've got an opportunity"'. *The Athletic*, 27 October. Available at https://theathletic.co.uk/2157211/2020/10/28/hope-powell-interview-black-history-month/.

7 Powell, H, *The Coaches' Voice*.

8 Powell, H, p247.

9 Powell, H, pp12–13.

10 Powell, H, pp69–70.

THE ANTI-FOOTBALLER

1 *All or Nothing: Tottenham Hotspur* (2019) 72 Films. Available at https://www.amazon.co.uk/All-or-Nothing-Tottenham-Hotspur/dp/B08G1YYZYN.

2 Romeo, C. (2017) Children at football academies are more likely to 'get hit by a meteorite' than succeed as professionals – here's the shocking statistic. *Business Insider*, 29 June. Available at

https://www.businessinsider.com/michael-calvin-shocking-statistic-why-children-football-academies-will-never-succeed-soccer-sport-2017–6?r=US&IR=T.

3 The Royal Family. (2019) *A Royal Team Talk: Tackling Mental Health 2019*. 20 May. Available at https://www.youtube.com/watch?v=Yn_shQZz5tw.

4 Delaney, M. (2018) Danny Rose: 'England is my salvation from my battle with depression. I'm the luckiest player in the World Cup squad'. *The Independent*, 6 June. Available at https://www.independent.co.uk/sport/football/world-cup/danny-rose-depression-england-world-cup-2018-gareth-southgate-family-a8386666.html.

5 Crafton, A. (2019) 'Dad came to watch me play a game and it cost him his life' – football's uneasy relationship with grief. *The Athletic*, 11 September. Available at https://theathletic.co.uk/1201003/2019/09/12/grief/.

6 The Royal Family, *A Royal Team Talk*.

7 Butler, P (2019). 'I could have shot you in front of your fucking kids': how cops dehumanize black people. *The Guardian*, 29 June. Available at https://www.theguardian.com/commentisfree/2019/jun/28/i-could-have-shot-you-in-front-of-your-fucking-kids-how-cops-dehumanize-black-people.

8 Platell, A. (2018) Platell's People: Can't you show a scintilla of gratitude, Stormzy? *Mail Online,* 24 February. Available at https://www.dailymail.co.uk/debate/article-5429041/Platells-People-Stormzy-gratitude.html.

9 Sadlier, R, and Early, K. (2020) Episode 1825: *The Player's Chair* with Danny Rose [Podcast]. Available at https://www.secondcaptains.com/2020/08/03/episode-1825-the-players-chair-with-danny-rose/.

10 Dapaah-Danquah, K (2019). The CARICOM guide to Black male mental health. *CARICOM* magazine issue 2, p22.

11 Hytner, D. (2019) Danny Rose 'can't wait to see the back' of football because of racism. *The Guardian,* 4 April. Available at https://www.theguardian.com/football/2019/apr/04/danny-rose-football-racism-england-tottenham.

12 Lewis, D. (2019) Tottenham's Danny Rose so sick of football racism he can't wait to retire. *The Mirror*, 4 April. Available at https://www.mirror.co.uk/sport/football/news/tottenhams-danny-rose-sick-football-14237563.

13 Thomas, L. (2019) Danny Rose says doing coaching badges are 'waste of time' because black players 'not given a chance'. *Sky*

Sports, 27 April. Available at https://www.skysports.com/football/news/11095/11704409/danny-rose-lost-for-words-over-montenegros-punishment-for-racist-abuse-of-england-players.

14 BBC Sport. (2019) 'Danny Rose has a responsibility to be an inspiration for young black players' – Jermaine Jenas. *BBC Sport*, 5 April. Available at https://www.bbc.co.uk/sport/football/47834993.

15 The School of Life. (2015) *The Wisdom of Pessimism.* 26 October. Available at https://www.youtube.com/watch?v=5jADnNpx3R4&feature=emb_title.

16 *Open Culture.* (2015) The power of pessimism: science reveals the hidden virtues in negative thinking. *Open Culture*, 12 November. Available at https://www.openculture.com/2015/11/the-power-of-pessimism-science-reveals-the-hidden-virtues-in-negative-thinking.html.

17 Channel 4 News. (2019) *George the Poet on Youth Violence, Representation, and Limitations of Government.* 24 July. Available at https://www.youtube.com/watch?v=pKwpjsWN8ow&t=1232s.

18 Andrews, K. (2018) *Back to Black: Retelling Black Radicalism for the 21st Century.* London: Zed Books.

19 247HH.COM. (2019) *Jidenna – Getting Evicted Led to Moving to Africa & Our Abusive Relationship With America.* 21 November. Available at https://www.youtube.com/watch?v=oCeshCHWAlU.

A PARALLEL HISTORY OF BLACK MUSLIM FOOTBALLERS

1 Taylor, L. (2011) Demba Ba marks his Newcastle arrival with hat-trick against Blackburn. *The Guardian*, 25 September. Available at https://www.theguardian.com/football/2011/sep/25/demba-ba-newcastle-blackburn.

2 MrBeanyman. (2021) Leicester 3–0 West Brom – Brendan Rodgers – post-match press conference. 21 April. Available at https://www.youtube.com/watch?v=6Nh3buw-G4E&ab_channel=MrBeanyman.

3 *The Muslim Premier League.* (2013) BBC One.

4 *The Guardian.* (2004) Kanoute cleared for Mali. *The Guardian*, 8 January. Available at https://www.theguardian.com/football/2004/jan/08/newsstory.sport2.

5 Guillem Balagué. (2021) *Can We Come In, FREDDIE KANOUTÉ? | Pure Football Podcast.* 20 March. Available at https://www.youtube.com/watch?v=daCD2_n4ebM.

6 Savvas, L. (2018) N'Golo Kante: Chelsea star eats curry and watches *Match of the Day* at fan's house after mosque meeting. *BBC Sport*, 17 September. https://www.bbc.co.uk/sport/football/45551585.

7 Channel 4 News. (2018) Jürgen Klopp interview: on Mo Salah, motivation, Brexit, how to win and how to lose. 23 April. Available at https://www.youtube.com/watch?v=a5bnJUaZwNc&ab_channel=Channel4News.

SOUTH LONDON SOIL

1 Wright, I (2018). Earning my smile. *The Players' Tribune*, 26 November. Available at https://www.theplayerstribune.com/articles/ian-wright-earning-my-smile.

2 Leighton, J. (2016) *Rocky: The Tears and Triumphs of David Rocastle*. London: Simon & Schuster UK.

3 Moody, G. (2013) Crystal Palace buy Beckenham training ground for £2.3m. *Sutton & Croydon Guardian*, 9 July. Available at https://www.yourlocalguardian.co.uk/sport/10535837.crystal-palace-buy-beckenham-training-ground-for-23m/.

4 Taylor, D. (2017) Gareth Southgate wanted Wilfried Zaha for England role but was too late. *The Guardian*, 27 March. Available at https://www.theguardian.com/football/2017/mar/27/wilfried-zaha-england-gareth-southgate-ivory-coast.

5 Sky Sports Football. (2018) *'I don't need to leave Crystal Palace' | Alex Scott Meets Wilfried Zaha*. 26 August. Available at https://www.youtube.com/watch?v=Mo4Ov3DAFGw&t=2s&ab_channel=SkySportsFootball.

6 *Rollin' Reds*. (2013) Wilfried Zaha interview. *Rollin' Reds*. Available at https://mudsa.org.uk/wilfred-zaha-interview/.

7 Everest, T. (2019) The calling: Eddie Nketiah. *The Gaffer*. Available at https://gaffer.online/features/football/the-calling-eddie-nketiah/.

8 Shearer, A. (2020) Alan Shearer meets Eddie Nketiah: England, Arteta, Bielsa and the joy of goals. *The Athletic*, 20 November. Available at https://theathletic.co.uk/2211031/2020/11/21/alan-shearer-eddie-nketiah/.

9 Arsenal. (2018) *EDDIE NKETIAH: Exclusive in-depth interview*. 15 January. Available at https://www.youtube.com/watch?v=2VF8eBqr8FQ&ab_channel=Arsenal.

A PORTRAIT IN ABSENCE

1 Hall, S. (2017) *The Fateful Triangle: Race, Ethnicity, Nation*. London: Harvard University Press, ix.

2 Serpell, N [@namwalien]. (2020) [Twitter] 20 January. Available at https://twitter.com/namwalien/status/1219328731757432835.
3 Roberts, A. (2008) Nelson Mandela is a hero, but not a saint. *The Guardian*, 26 June. Available at https://www.theguardian.com/commentisfree/2008/jun/26/nelsonmandela.zimbabwe.
4 Campbell, A. (2019) How it feels to ... talk to Raheem Sterling about racist abuse. *The Times*, 24 July. Available at https://www.thetimes.co.uk/article/how-it-feels-to-talk-to-raheem-sterling-about-racist-abuse-mwvkhqzxq.
5 Carrington, B. (2010) *Race, Sport and Politics: the Sporting Black Diaspora*. London: SAGE Publications, p104.
6 Northcroft, J. (2020) Raheem Sterling: 'The perception that footballers are all selfish and money-driven has changed'. *The Sunday Times*, 25 October. Available at https://www.thetimes.co.uk/article/raheem-sterling-interview-charity-perception-footballers-selfish-money-driven-93fb77pwq.
7 Onuora, E. (2015) *Pitch Black: the Story of Black British Footballers*. Hull: Biteback Publishing, xix.
8 Andrews, K. (2018) *Back to Black: Retelling Black Radicalism for the 21st Century*. London: Zed Books, p27.
9 *Blacks Britannica* (1978) Directed by D Koff. Available at https://www.youtube.com/watch?v=lsKeRFpyKNw&app=desktop&ab_channel=bagheera.
10 Hinds, D. (1966) *Journey to an Illusion*. London: Heinemann.
11 Grant, C. (2020) *Homecoming*. London: Vintage.
12 *Desert Island Discs* (2020) BBC Radio 4: Broadcast 16 October 09:00.
13 The New School (2015) *bell hooks and Kevin Powell: Black Masculinity, Threat or Threatened*. 7 October. Available at https://www.youtube.com/watch?v=FoXNzyK70Bk&ab_channel=TheNewSchool.
14 Northcroft, J, *The Sunday Times*.
15 Hiro, D. (1971) *Black British, White British*. London: Eyre & Spottiswoode, p67.
16 Jackson, J. (2017) Raheem Sterling: 'I've got that face people don't like but I'm not a brat'. *The Guardian*, 31 March. Available at https://www.theguardian.com/football/2017/mar/31/raheem-sterling-manchester-city-im-not-a-brat.
17 Hall, S. (2018) *Familiar Stranger: A Life Between Two Islands*. 2nd edn. London: Penguin, p211.
18 Hall, S, *Familiar Stranger*, p204.
19 Jackson, J, *The Guardian*.

20 This article has since disappeared from the internet but is referenced by Musa Okwonga in his review of Emy Onuora's book *Pitch Black*. Okwonga, M. (2015) Red card to racists: Graham Taylor was told not to pick too many black players for England. *New Statesman*, 7 May. Available at https://www.newstatesman.com/2015/05/red-card-racists-graham-taylor-was-told-not-pick-too-many-black-players-england.

21 Gilroy, P. (2001) Foreword, in Carrington, B, and McDonald, I (eds). *'Race', Sport and British Society*. London: Routledge, xvi.

Acknowledgements

I am immensely grateful to my friends Candice, Diogo, Ellen, Emma, Gena, George, Eli, Jamila, Jerome, Joey, Lola, Maude, Milo, Musa, Nigel, Owen, Ryan and Sanaa. I will never forget the love, care and practical support you extended to me throughout this process and a difficult time in my life. I wouldn't have made it this far without you all.

I would also like to thank Odhran O'Donoghue, Daniel Harris and George Webster for their editorial support.

A special mention must go to my brother, Luke, who ensured that football was always on in our home and never once shied away from challenging the received wisdom of the press.

Last, but by no means least, the opportunity to write this book arose in large part because of the work I produced in *CARICOM Magazine*. So, to anyone who collaborated with me, backed the Kickstarters I initiated, bought a copy of the magazine, showed up to an event or simply told friends and family about the publication, I want you to know that I'm continually thankful to you too.

Picture Permissions

Nottingham Forest v West Bromwich Albion – Football League Division One © Paul Popper/Popperfoto

Justin and John Fashanu, February 1981 © Manchester Daily Express

Justin Fashanu, British footballer, c 1980s © Manchester Daily Express

Leicester v Arsenal © Mark Leech/Offside

Sport. Football. pic: 13th April 1997. Division 1. Arsenal v Bolton Wanderers. Arsenal striker Ian Wright celebrates after breaking the club's goal-scoring record (in fact he celebrated one goal too early, but later in the game went on to complete a hat-trick) © Bob Thomas

Friday Night's All Wright TV Show, Britain, 1999. Ian Wright, Sir Trevor McDonald © Ken McKay/Shutterstock

Volume 2. Page: 12. Picture 1. Sport. Football. 1994 World Cup Qualifier. Bologna, Italy. 17th November, 1993. San Marino 1 v England 7. A rear view of the England players in the tunnel to take the field for the second half © Bob Thomas

Sport. Football. FIFA Club World Championships. Rio De Janeiro, Brazil. 11th January, 2000. Manchester United 2 v South Melbourne 0. Manchester United's captain for the day Andy Cole gives an interview after the game © Bob Thomas

Sport, Football, pic: 1994–1995, Newcastle United striker Andy Cole on the ball © Bob Thomas

Juventus v Manchester United © John Peters

Hope Powell © Clive Brunskill

England Women Training & Press Conference © Ian Walton

Arsenal FC 'Iconic' Archive © David Price

Czech Republic v England – UEFA Euro 2020 Qualifier © Justin Setterfield

Ajax v Tottenham Hotspur – UEFA Champions League © Soccrates Images

Newcastle United v West Bromwich Albion – Premier League © Ian T. Horrocks

Sevilla's Luis Fabiano (R) celebrates with Frédéric Kanouté (L) © CRISTINA QUICLER/AFP via Getty Images

Chelsea v Leicester City: The Emirates FA Cup Final © Eddie Keogh – The FA

West Bromwich Albion v Southend United © Clive Brunskill

Kevin Campbell, Michael Thomas, David Rocastle, Kevin Campbell and Paul Davis © Colorsport

Crystal Palace v Leicester City © Christopher Lee

Charlton 1 Fulham 1 – 09 Sep 2001. Jason Euell – Charlton Charlton Athletic v Fulham FA Premiership 9/9/01 Great Britain London © Andrew Cowie/Shutterstock

England Under-17 Photo Call © Laurence Griffiths – The FA

Manchester United v Manchester City – Carabao Cup Semi Final © Matt McNulty – Manchester City

Contributor Biographies

Calum Jacobs is a British-Guyanese writer, editor, and creative practitioner from south London who draws on sociology, history and culture to explore the liminality of Black British life. In 2017, he launched *CARICOM Magazine*, a print and online platform dedicated to discussing football and broader culture through a Black lens. Jacobs is also a contributor to various sport and culture publications, and has worked on creative projects for agencies and brands. *A New Formation* is his first book.
Instagram: @caricomweb @badcal
Twitter: @caricomweb

Musa Okwonga is the author of two books on football, the first of which was nominated for the 2008 William Hill Sports Book of the Year award, and one collection of poetry. He is the co-founder and co-host of the *Stadio* football podcast, and his memoir about his five years at Eton College, *One of Them*, was published in 2021.
Instagram: @okwonga
Twitter: @okwonga

Thomas Theodore is a writer, musician and lifelong Arsenal fan based in Islington, London.
Instagram: @teddy.slendergrass

Jude Wanga is a writer, activist and editor at *New Socialist.*
Twitter: @judewanga

Jeanette Kwakye MBE is a five-time British athletics champion and was a finalist in the 100 metres Olympic final in Beijing in 2008. She is now an experienced sports broadcaster and journalist for the BBC, Sky and Channel 5. Jeanette also works with young people in schools on behalf of the Youth Sport Trust.
Instagram: @justjnette
Twitter: @jnettekwakye

Kwaku Dapaah-Danquah is a British-Ghanaian entrepreneur, podcaster and programme manager with interests spanning personal development and social enterprise. His podcast *Over the Bridge* won an award in the Acast Moment of the Year category at the 2019 British Podcast Awards for its feature interview of Stormzy. Kwaku has written frequently on identity and wellbeing for his own blog, as well as contributing to issue two of *CARICOM*, with a pamphlet insert on Black male mental health.
Instagram: @kwakudapaah_
Twitter: @kwakudapaah_

Sanaa Qureshi is a project manager in community sport who lives in London. She has contributed to *Unusual Efforts*, *MUNDIAL* magazine, *Stadio*, *Popula* and *Khidr Zine*.
Instagram: @sanaaqureshi
Twitter: @sanaa_mq

Aniefiok 'Neef' Ekpoudom is a writer from South London who documents and explores culture in Britain. In his work, Aniefiok tells stories about the people and movements shaping the country as it exists today. He has written for, and worked with, *The Guardian*, British *GQ*, British *Vogue*, *The Observer*,

GRM Daily, Adidas, Nike, Netflix UK, and more. His first book, *Where We Come From*, will be released via Faber & Faber in 2023.
Instagram: @aniefiokekp
Twitter: @aniefiokekp